THE OPENING
OF THE
AMERICAN WEST

IN EARLY PHOTOGRAPHS AND PRINTS

THE OPENING
OF THE
AMERICAN WEST

GENERAL EDITOR: BILL YENNE

CHARTWELL
BOOKS, INC.

Published by
CHARTWELL BOOKS, INC.
A Division of **BOOK SALES, INC.**
110 Enterprise Avenue
Secaucus, New Jersey 07094

Produced by
Brompton Books Corp.
15 Sherwood Place
Greenwich, CT 06830

ISBN 1-55521-870-9

Printed in Hong Kong

Designed by Bill Yenne

The editors wish to extend their thanks to Richard F Weingroff of the Federal Highway Administration for his indispensable assistance in the research for the final chapter of this book.

Page 2: **An early photographer at work near Glacier Point high above Yosemite Valley in California's Sierra Nevada range. Yosemite Falls, fed by winter snowpack, thunders in the background.**

Photo Credits

AGS Archives 1, 10, 16, 22, 23, 23, 25, 26, 30, 31, 32, 35, 36, 40, 52, 55, 62, 68, 71 (right), 74, 104, 144, 149 (both), 156, 157, 58, 183, 185, 187
FA Ames Collection, National Archives 50, 51
Bancroft Library 65, 171, 172, 173
Bureau of Illustration 150 (top)
California State Library 28, 61, 66-67, 118, 140, 188, 189, 192
Colt Firearms 42, 43
John Hillers Collection, National Archives 12
William H Jackson Collection, National Archives 78, 81, 107, 108 (top), 114 (bottom), 115, 116, 177
Kilburn & Cross 38, 54, 63, 72, 106, 114 (top), 144, 146, 152, 160, 162
Library of Congress 2, 85, 95, 145, 151
Los Angeles County Museum 42-43, 64
National Archives 4, 7, 8, 13, 14, 19, 20, 27, 29, 33, 37, 39, 40-41, 44, 45, 46, 47, 48, 49, 56, 57, 58, 59, 67, 71 (left), 73, 75, 76, 77, 79, 80, 84, 86, 108 (bottom), 109, 110 (both), 112, 117, 118-119, 129, 147, 150

(bottom), 153, 154, 155 (both), 159, 163, 164, 165, 166, 167, 168, 169, 170, 174, 175, 176, 178, 179, 180, 181, 183, 184, 186
National Railway Historical Society 53
Timothy O'Sullivan Collection, National Archives 11, 13, 34, 111, 113
San Francisco Archives 21, 69
Smithsonian Institution, National Anthropological Archives 128, 132, 139 (bottom)
South Dakota Historical Society 138 (right, both), 139 (top, both)
Southern Pacific Railroad 88 (right), 90, 91, 92, 93, 94, 96, 98, 99, 100, 102, 105
Union Pacific Railroad 17, 87, 88 (left), 89, 97, 101, 103
Utah State Historical Society 82-83
University of Nevada at Reno 141 (both)
US Army Signal Corps via National Archives 120, 121, 122, 123, 124, 125, 126, 127, 130, 131 (both), 133 (both), 134, 135, 136, 137, 138 (left), 142, 143
Vandercook E&P Company 60, 70

Below: **A view of Gardiner, Montana, looking northeast, as it appeared in 1887. Note the one-sided street backed up to the rocky foothills.**

Table of Contents

PREFACE

by Dr Howard R Driggs

One cannot better describe that great highway of humanity that began in the cradle of civilization in the time of Abraham and concluded on the shores of the Pacific over the Pioneer Oregon Trail, than in the memorial address given over a century ago by Dr Howard R Driggs on the death of Ezra Meeker, one of the foremost of the pioneer leaders.

It touches closely every part of our country, North, South, East and West. Every state in the Union has an heroic son or daughter who has played a valiant part in the trail-blazing, home-building story of the West.

What is the West? It is merely the transplanted East. It is the blended North and South. We sometimes hear the song 'Out Where the West Begins.' Frankly, I do not know where the West begins, but I *do* know where it began. It began along the shores of the stormy Atlantic. Our American pioneers were descendants of those who planted our 13 American colonies and who afterward fought to establish this nation dedicated to freedom. It was the descendants of these stalwart defenders of liberty who carried America westward. They followed the Indian trails through the passes of the Allegheny Mountains along the national highways to the Mississippi. They wended their way over the prairies and plains and mountains and deserts to the shores of the Pacific, there to plant American states beyond the Rockies.

It is not commonly known how great this migration was. We get a mere suggestion of it when we learn from conservative estimates that fully 350,000 Americans took these trails during the days of the covered wagon–from 1843, when Marcus Whitman and his wife first made their way to Oregon, to 1869, when the Golden Spike linking the Union Pacific and the Central Pacific was driven at Promontory, at the north end of the Great Salt Lake in Utah.

We are brought a little closer to the tragic cost of it all when we realize that fully 20,000 lost their lives in the effort to reach the golden West. Somewhere among the velvety hills of old Iowa, four of my great-grandparents lie in unmarked graves. They had no means of marking the graves of the dead in those prairie stretches. They might have put the skull of a buffalo, the end gate of a wagon or some other temporary marker, at the mound of the loved one laid away, but mainly what they did was to scatter the ashes of their campfires over these resting places to keep the bodies of their dear ones from being dug up by the wolves.

Only one grave out of all of the 20,000, so far as we know, is surely marked. I refer here to the grave of the pioneer mother near Scott's Bluffs, Nebraska. When Rebecca Winters passed away, one of the company had the happy forethought to pick up an old

Above: The first homesteaders' wagons leaving the line north of Orlando for Perry in Oklahoma Territory on 16 September 1893.

Right: This stage of the Concord type, as seen in this 1869 photograph, was typical of those used by the express companies on the overland trails.

Facing page: By 1826, the major cities on, or east of, the Mississippi, such as Chicago, St Louis, Memphis, New Orleans and Mobile, were already in place. West of the Mississippi, however, the continent was still largely a wilderness with vast sections written off to Indian tribes.

The Great Salt Lake had been discovered by several independent expeditions, and people still thought there were *two* huge lakes, Timpanogos and Salado.

The Timpanogos River and the Buenaventura River were still thought to originate in these lakes because no-one had discovered the Sierra Nevada yet. No water can flow from Utah to California because of the Sierra Nevada. Now known as the Eel and the Sacramento, these rivers actually originate in the Sierra.

wagon tire that lay along the trail. Bending it into an oval he set the tire within the grave. On the top of the tire was chiseled the mother's name and age. For more than 30 years, it stood over the mound. Finally a party of surveyors laying out a railroad along the old North Platte happened to run their line right over the mother's grave by chance because it was on the old Salt Lake branch of the Oregon Trail. As they read the inscription on the old wagon tire, they were touched by the love of a mother's heart. They telegraphed into Salt Lake City, and relatives of the pioneer mother wired back who she was. With a touch of sympathy that is beautiful to think upon, the surveyors went back for 20 miles and changed the line of survey, so that it would miss Rebecca Winters' grave.

George Hines, secretary of the Oregon Historical Association, told the story of the pioneers coming into the then Territory of Washington when he was a boy of 10, as his family traveled into the far Northwest when they had to kill three of their oxen to use their hides to splice two ropes to let their 29 wagons down a cliff that barred their way.

Mr Hines showed me during this visit one of the corners of the museum in which he had relics that had come from every state east of the Mississippi River. 'Here,' he said, 'is a clock that used to tick time in Vermont. Here is a Franklin stove with which they used to warm themselves in Pennsylvania. Here is a cradle in which they rocked the baby across the plains from Indiana, and here is a scythe with which they mowed blue grass in Kentucky.'

'Yes, Mr Hines' I replied, 'these people came bearing not only their scythes and their stoves, their clocks and their cradles, they came carrying America across our continent. They came sprinkling the names of American towns and cities dear to their hearts upon the map of every state that they crossed. They came planting their school houses and churches. They came telling their children of the making of America. They came with American ideals throbbing in their hearts. They came, if you please, stretching the warp of our national life from one end of our country to the other. They stretched it stout and taut and true.'

The opening of the American West was an enormous achievement. Americans accomplished in 100 years what neither Europe nor Asia had achieved in 4000. The Overland Trail, the Oregon Trail, the Santa Fe Trail and the California Trail may together be regarded from end to end as the fulfillment of that divine prophecy 'when His dominions shall extend from the rivers to the ends of the earth.' It would be beautified, revered and consecrated as a great national highway.

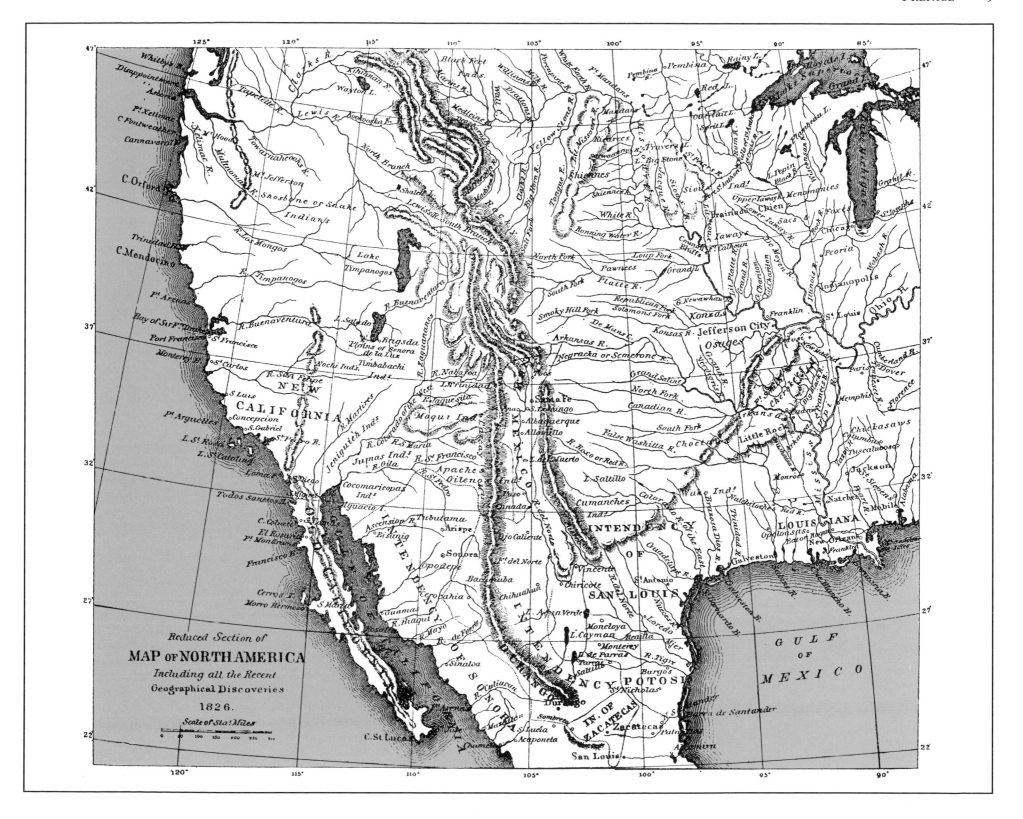

Reduced Section of
MAP of NORTH AMERICA
*Including all the Recent
Geographical Discoveries*
1826.

Scale of Stat! Miles

INTRODUCTION

Above: The adobe dwellings of the Zuni and other Pueblo Indians were a disappointment to the Spaniards who had heard legends of cities made of gold.

Facing page: A member of Clarence King's Geological Exploration of the fortieth parallel surveying from a rock in Shoshone Canyon in Idaho Territory, as photographed by Timothy O'Sullivan in 1868.

No element of America's historical heritage has inspired more myth and more legend than the opening of the American West. As Dr Driggs points out in his preface, settling the West was an accomplishment of monumental proportions carried out by people of sturdy countenance and far-reaching vision.

What then was the West, this great land that was brought into the nation by the pioneers of the nineteenth century? As Dr Driggs points out, the drive westward began on the shores of the Atlantic with the first European pioneers who arrived in the beginning of the seventeenth century. After the birth of the nation, the notion of the West was embodied in the lands immediately beyond the borders of the original 13 states. This area, which lay beyond the Appalachian Mountains, was opened by men like Daniel Boone, who led the first pioneers through the Cumberland Gap.

The West of our national legend, however, began at the Mississippi River, that 2348-mile-long demarcation line which still divides our national identity and defines our roles within our national legend. It flows through a billion-acre area that still contains the least densely populated states in the Union. For example, Wyoming's population density, as reflected in the 1990 census, was less than that of Alaska.

In the nineteenth century, the area beyond the Mississippi was a *terra incognita* known as the Great American Desert—a forbidding, uncharted (or barely charted) wilderness of parched landscapes inhabited by wild animals and native people who were considered as 'savages.' It was also seen as a land of promise and a gateway to the Pacific Coast, a region regarded as a wonderland at the end of the rainbow.

Even as late as the 1840s, when the cities and states of the Atlantic seaboard enjoyed the all the accoutrements of 'civilization'—ranging from steam locomotives and daily newspapers, to the elegance and refinement of a well-established social structure—the West was still seen as being barely past the Stone Age. Most of its more than one billion acres were known only to roving trappers and fur traders, and of course locally to the various tribes of natives.

The West was indeed a land of mystery. No accurate map existed—no map *at all* of a great portion—and many of its salient characteristics were as yet unfathomed. This was

Above: **In 1872, under the auspices of the Smithsonian Institution, John Wesley Powell undertook a general survey of the West. His chief photographer was John K Hillers, seen at work with his negatives at the expedition's camp on the Aquarius Plateau, Utah Territory.**

Facing page: **Timothy O'Sullivan's ambulance wagon and portable darkroom, used during the 1867 King Geographic Survey, rolls across the sand dunes of Carson Desert, Nevada.**

especially true of the area spreading between the Wasatch and the Sierra Nevada, south of the Snake River, which was largely uninvestigated, though several trapping parties had ventured within its desolate expanse. Jedediah Smith had crossed the desert valleys to and from California twice between 1826 and 1828, and in 1833, Joseph Walker had gone down the Humboldt and over the Sierra Nevada to Monterey, then back the next year by a more southern course.

The general topographic features encountered in going westward from the Missouri across the immense new country were first the Great Plains, with an average elevation above the sea of about two thousand feet, considered by Pike, Long and other prominent men of the early quarter of the nineteenth century to be a 'Great American Desert,' which they believed would forever form an effective barrier between the settlements of the United States and those of Mexico. This 'desert' vanished as a barrier, of course, but in the beginning the plains actually offered a considerable obstacle to exploration. They rolled away to the beckoning West, mile upon mile like a mighty petrified sea, to the very foothills of the second repelling barrier, the imposing, ponderous chain of the Rocky Mountains extending northerly and southerly across the heart of the wilderness, dividing it into almost equal parts.

At the center of this great interior mountain system, six long rivers find their source: the Columbia, the Colorado, the Rio Grande, the Arkansas, the Platte (described as a thousand miles long and nine inches deep) and the mighty Missouri. These streams, beginning so near together, immediately diverge, and four of them sweep away to different seas. Each, therefore, possesses an enormous valley or drainage basin.

Prior to 1830, other great rivers were imagined to exist in the region west of Salt Lake, the Buenaventura, taking its rise in the Rocky Mountains and flowing westward through a 'Lake Salado' to the Bay of San Francisco, evidently based on the Sevier, the Rio Timpanogos and the Rio Los Mongos, based roughly on the Humboldt, and perhaps on the Owyhee, or possibly on an imagined eastward extension of Oregon's Rogue River. Both of the latter fabulous streams were supposed to rise in a 'Lake Timpanogos' (an imaginary Utah Lake originally, whose name was later applied to Salt Lake). On the map of North America by A Finley (Philadelphia, 1826), the three mythical rivers are confidently drawn from source to finish, though maps of earlier date do not show them.

It was the journeys of Jedediah Smith (1826-1828) and of Joseph Walker (1833-1834) which eliminated the mythical rivers. Senator Thomas Hart Benton claimed the honor for his son-in-law, the great explorer John Charles Fremont. It hardly belongs directly to him, though it may be said that until Fremont traversed the country there was no definite scientific decision on the matter, and *after* his expedition, nothing was possible to the most active imagination.

Following these came the immediate valley of the formidable Colorado River, one of the most extraordinary features of the West. The Colorado was the most effective barrier of all against exploration because it included a line of deep, barren, rock-bound chasms called in Spanish *cañons* (in English, the *ñ* being rendered *ny*). These included the Grand Canyon and Marble Canyon, which combined were 283 miles long and reached a depth of between 5000 and 6000 feet and a width of more than 12 miles. These canyons were cut by the river and presented, for about 1000 miles, as difficult an obstruction to the traveler as could be devised. It was only at a few places far apart that a practicable passage from one side to the other existed. Together with the aridness of the region and consequent scarcity of springs, these canyons, from whose precipitous cliffs

Above: In 1899, E Jay Haynes photographed holiday passengers arriving at the Hot Springs Hotel in South Dakota. American flags flap in the breeze. The stagecoaches were met by other vacationers on the hotel veranda.

Facing page: William Jennings Bryan and Governor Lee in Wind Cave, South Dakota, 350 feet below the surface at the Odd Fellows Hall. The photograph was taken by WR Cross in 1897.

one might hear the roar of the river and even plainly see its seething waters while dying of thirst, presented an appalling obstacle. They were universally dreaded and avoided, and fearful tales of their dangers and mysteries were in vogue.

Farther west came the splendid summits of the Wasatch, the fourth barrier, which in itself formed the eastern rim of the fifth barrier, the Great Basin. The sixth, and last, great barrier is the stupendous snowy chain of the Sierra Nevada, the 'White Saw.'

The Sierra Nevada is a range of extreme grandeur and beauty, and some of its valleys, like the Yosemite and the Hetch-Hetchy (until it was dammed to provide water for the city of San Francisco) were among the most majestic spectacles of the world. Beyond the Sierra Nevada are the long, central, fruitful valleys of the San Joaquin and the Sacramento, which form the fertile heart of California. To the west, these valleys are guarded by another range, parallel with the coast, and consequently called the Coast Range. The Coast and the Sierra Nevada ranges unite near the fortieth parallel and together they extend northward as the Cascade Range. All the country east of this Sierra Nevada Range has relatively little rainfall, but owing to the large number of mountains, snow run-off provides for many permanent rivers and creeks whose waters are now utilized for irrigation.

Wildlife was plentiful in the vast lands of the West. On the plains, and ranging across the Rocky Mountains as far as Green River and the head of Snake River, there roamed herds of buffalo, and when the beaver, which first tempted the European into the wilderness, began to diminish in numbers, the buffalo were more specially hunted, until at last they were slaughtered by the thousands merely for their hides, tallow and tongues.

There were also bear in abundance, the grizzly being the most dangerous. In the early days, the grizzly was virtually invincible against the low-powered, muzzle-loading rifles which trappers used. Hence its reputation led to its Latin name *ursus horribilis*. Almost every other kind of animal known on this continent was also found here: deer, elk, mountain sheep, goats, mountain lions, wild cats, wolves, lynx, rabbits, pine and sage hens, grouse, turkeys, quail, trout and other fish, lizards of many sizes up to the poisonous, two-foot-long Gila monster, and other creatures, such as scorpions, centipedes, tarantulas, several species of rattlesnake, and, on the Pacific coast, seals and sea lions.

In the way of vegetation, there were some extraordinary species to keep pace with the animals. The most remarkable are the giant redwoods that grow in the Sierra Nevada and on the California coast.

The human population was large but widely scattered. The Great Plains were dominated by Native American tribes such as the Sioux, the Cheyenne, the Crow, the Arapaho and the Blackfoot which had portable tepees. The Shoshone occupied the district from the crest or divide of the Rocky Mountains to the Sierra Nevada, while below that parallel were two groups of Athapascans, Apache and Navajo, with various tribes known as Pueblos (or Puebloans). The Puebloans dwelt in substantial houses, constructed of stone, or of sun-dried brick known as adobe, in valleys, canyons and on the summits of cliff-bound tables known as mesas. At the same time, there were innumerable ruins of former habitations, specifically the Anasazi of Canyon de Chelly and Mesa Verde.

The native villages of the Southwest possessed actual permanent settlements long before the arrival of the Europeans, and when they finally came in search of fabulous riches and 'The Seven Cities,' these little towns, ungilded and unadorned, were a

Above: When the great buffalo herds still roamed the plains, early western locomotives used water spouting devices to chase them off the tracks.

Facing page: Joining the tracks for the first transcontinental railroad at Promontory in Utah Territory on 10 March 1869.

disappointment. Yet over the years, such villages became welcome places of refuge for many a trapper or hunter where he could obtain food and shelter, without price if necessary. The Puebloans had plenty of maize, watermelons, beans and squash. Hospitality was a part of the Indian custom destroyed by the neglect or refusal of the whites to reciprocate.

Although various solitary trappers and adventurers had penetrated the Great American Desert for nearly a century, the 1804-1806 expedition by Meriwether Lewis and William Clark was the first organized American expedition to cross the continent from the Mississippi to the Pacific Ocean.

After them, the first systematic effort by the US government to survey the West was during the expeditions undertaken by John Charles Fremont (1813-1890), the charismatic explorer known as 'the Pathfinder.' Fremont was a young engineer attached to the Army in 1842 when he was sent to survey the South Pass in the Rockies. In 1843 and 1844, he was again ordered to the Far West, this time to the Columbia River country, from which he returned by way of California and a southern trail. In 1845, he was on the margin of the Spanish settlements when the Bear Flag Revolt (California's 'war of independence' from Mexico) broke out in 1846, and he placed himself at the head of the American settlers who cooperated with the Army and the Navy in the conquest of California.

With the trails in operation, Indian lands were doomed. In 1849, the California gold rush broke all records for migration, and active mining camps began calling for government protection from marauders. In the great Missouri Compromise of 1850, California entered the Union as a state and Oregon, Utah and New Mexico as territories. Four years later, with the repeal of the Compromise, the Kansas and Nebraska territories were carved from Indian lands, reducing the latter to the dimensions of the present state of Oklahoma.

In 1858, the famous Overland Mail service, with stagecoaches running from Missouri to California, made its appearance. The traveler in one of these vehicles could expect to spend nearly three weeks in the cramped quarters of a Concord coach, with little sleep and poor food provided at the stations where the horses were changed.

In 1860, the Pony Express began running from St Joseph, Missouri to Sacramento, California, with riders carrying tissue paper letters in their saddlebags, rushing through on the fleetest ponies the owners could provide. It was while on this service that the young William 'Buffalo Bill' Cody learned about the Far West. When that the electric telegraph supplanted the Pony Express in 1861, Cody turned scout and hunter, and later became a famous showman. His image was for many years considered to be an important part of the legend of the West.

In 1869, remote sections of the United States were connected by the transcontinental railroad, and the importance of the wagon trails diminished. The completion of the transcontinental railroad in 1869 was a pivotal point in the opening of the American West, but it would be many years before the West was truly open. It was not until the 1890s that the Indian Wars finally ended in the arroyos of the Southwest and Congress declared an official end to the 'frontier' status of the West. Indeed, it was not until 5 November 1935 that it was possible to drive a car from coast to coast on a paved highway!

This, then, is the story—in words and pictures—of the brave men and women who pioneered trails through a vast wilderness, across seemingly insurmountable obstacles, to open the American West.

THE DEVELOPMENT OF THE OVERLAND TRAIL

Lewis and Clark (1804-1806)

Their explorations up the Three Forks and the Missouri rivers were extended into Nez Perce country in 1805. They reached the Pacific Ocean in 1805, and their return trip over the trail was made in 1806.

Astorians and Missouri Fur Traders (1811-1840)

The Astorians (people inspired by fur baron John Jacob Astor to settle in Oregon) made the terrible passage of the Snake River Canyon between 26 September 1811 and New Year's Day in 1812. They rested on the Umatilla River and reached the Columbia River on 21 January 1812. The rendezvous of the fur traders at Pierre's Hole, Jackson's Hole, and Henry's House, became stations for rest and repair of gear.

Fort Hall and Boise, Idaho's capital, grew from American and British posts in the fur war. After the Hudson's Bay Company and the Northwest Company of Montreal united in 1820, Peter Skene Ogden commanded their formidable forces until the trade lost its supremacy. Astoria, Oregon, situated at the mouth of the Columbia, is named for the Astorians.

Pioneers and Missionaries (1836-1856)

Gradually, as its use increased, the Oregon Trail was made more serviceable. Jim Bridger knew in the early 1830s that it was possible to get wagons across the Teton Mountains. However, Benjamin Louis Bonneville may have been the first to do it in 1832 or 1834. By 1843, wagon trains were in full parade.

The California Gold Rush (1848-1858)

Discovery of gold in the Sierra Nevada of California precipitated the greatest mass migration in American history. The California Trail over the mountains, pioneered by Fremont only a decade before, became a well-traveled thoroughfare.

The Transcontinental Railroads (1868-1893)

The Central Pacific Railroad, building east from California, crossed the Sierra Nevada in 1868. The Union Pacific Railroad, building west from Chicago, crossed the Rockies a year later, and when the two linked up at Promontory, Utah on 10 May 1869, the continent was bound once and for all by bands of steel.

The Atchison, Topeka & Santa Fe Railroad followed the old Santa Fe Trail to conclude a southern transcontinental rail route to southern California in 1881, and the Great Northern Railway was completed across a northern transcontinental route to Seattle in 1893.

Above: A 'boomers camp' in Arkansas County, Kansas. These people were waiting for the strip to open for homesteading on 1 March 1893.

Facing page: San Francisco's famous Seven Mile House offered cold steam beer, hot steamed clams, cigars and a ladies' sitting room to travellers in the 1860s.

THE FIRST PIONEERS

Above: John Fremont, 'the Great Pathfinder,' raising the flag on the tallest peak of the Rocky Mountains.

Facing page: Thomas Jeffreys drew this map of North America in 1782. It records the explorations made of the Pacific Coast including *(from top)* those by Vitus Bering (1741), Juan de Fuca (1542) and Sir Francis Drake (1578). Although he has drawn San Francisco Bay, Jeffreys insisted that Port Sir Francis Drake was *not* San Francisco Bay.

In fact, Drake is thought to have bypassed the Golden Gate and to have landed at what is now known as Drake's Bay, about 20 miles to the north.

The great Spanish conquistador Coronado himself traveled eastward almost to the present site of Kansas City. Within a half century, others followed to 'New Mexico,' and by 1680, numbers of Spaniards were living in the Rio Grande valley. The padres had founded missions and built substantial churches.

In 1680, the discontent of the Native Americans developed into a rebellion so well directed that every foreigner was either killed or driven from the territory. The Europeans were, in their own opinion, the only people with rights, and they soon returned with a more powerful military force. The Spaniards then remained masters of the region for 150 years, until 1848, when the United States annexed the region. Santa Fe was founded by Juan de Onate four years before Henry Hudson's discovery of Manhattan Island in 1605.

Meanwhile, the indomitable French were advancing from the northeast, and in 1682, three-quarters of a century after the Spaniards had settled in Santa Fe, Robert Cavalier de la Salle (1643-1687) came down the Mississippi and made the claim at its mouth to 'Louisiana' which included everything the Spaniards and British did not already hold.

In 1738, another French nobleman, Pierre Gaulthier de Varennes de la Verendrye, entered the West from the Manitoba region of Canada and explored as far south as the Mandan villages, near what is now Bismarck in North Dakota. His two sons arrived in 1742 and proceeded from the Mandans west and southwest to the Rocky Mountains, which they reached in the early part of 1743. It is probable that they went as far as Montana's Wind River range. In 1739, other Frenchmen journeyed a considerable distance up the South Platte, so the French, by right of exploration, had a strong hold on all the Mississippi Valley.

A half century later, in 1793, Sir Alexander Mackenzie (1764-1820) succeeded in crossing the continent by way of Peace River Pass and arrived on the shore of the Pacific Ocean not far from Queen Charlotte Sound. This was the first known crossing of the continent by a European north of Mexico. Reports of a very large 'River of the West,'–sometimes called the Oregon after a mention of it in Jonathan Carver's book– flowing to the western sea, figured on maps at least as early as 1753, though the

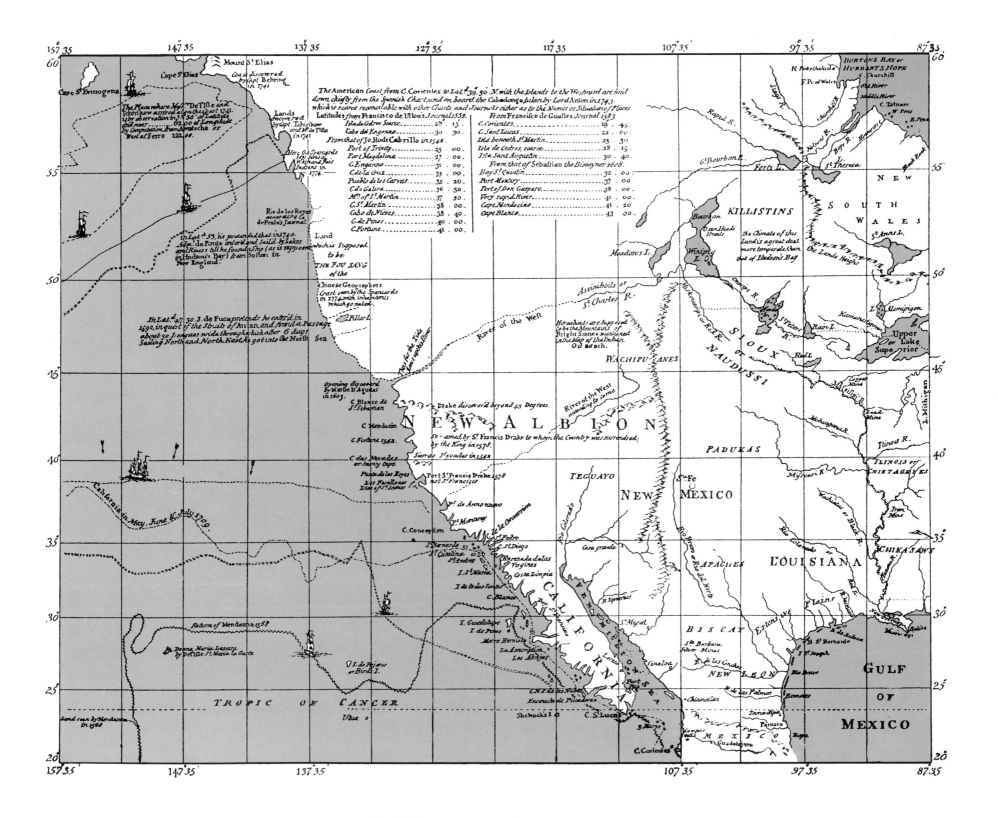

Right: Thomas Jefferson was one of the leading American proponents of Manifest Destiny as a national policy. He bought Louisiana from Napoleon and was anxious to see it explored. He would have liked to have gone with Lewis and Clark himself.

Facing page: This map shows the major geographical features of the American West, although they would not be fully mapped until after the expeditions of the early explorers. Depicted here are the routes taken by (1) Merriwether Lewis and William Clark in 1804-1806, (2) Zebulon Pike in 1806-1807 and (3) John Fremont–'the Great Pathfinder'– in 1842-1844.

location of its exit to the ocean could not be determined. It remained for an American trading captain, Robert Gray, to discover the mouth of the Columbia River. Gray sailed to the bar and put his ship through a passage in the breakers, discovered from the masthead, into the mouth of the beautiful river, naming it after his vessel which was the first to enter. This was a fortunate circumstance for the United States, as this discovery of the mouth of the River of the West became a strong point in the dispute over the ownership of Oregon.

At the close of the American Revolution, after independence had been won, the United States was a seaboard nation, with the Mississippi River as a western boundary. Pioneer settlements were located from Pittsburgh to St Louis. The rivers carried the canoes of the prospectors and the flatboats of the settlers into the wilderness. The cabins of the frontiersmen appeared in the clearings in the forest, and the clearings grew and spread until broad and fertile fields became common everywhere. Everywhere, that is, that was east of the Mississippi. There were few who worried over what lay beyond.

One of the founding fathers, and the third president of the United States, Thomas Jefferson was one of the few who worried. Immensely curious, he wanted to know where the Rocky Mountains were. He knew that the vast Missouri emptied into the Mississippi from the west just above the mouth of the Ohio, but no one could tell him where it originated. In 1803, it unexpectedly became possible to buy the whole of French Louisiana.

Napoleon needed the money and Jefferson recognized a unique opportunity to double the size of the United States. To Thomas Jefferson belongs the original idea of an American exploration into the Great West. Jefferson's interest went back to the infancy of the Republic. While ambassador to France, he met John Ledyard of Connecticut, who had accompanied Captain Cook on his voyage to the Pacific Ocean in 1778. Jefferson proposed to him an exploration of western America. The most notable feature of the plan adopted was that Ledyard was not to proceed *westward* from the United States, but was to cross Europe and Russian Asia to Kamchatka, board a Russian vessel to Nootka Sound, cross the mountains to the headwaters of the Missouri, and make his way eastward to the United States. Through the Russian minister at Paris, Jefferson secured assurances of protection from the empress of Russia for Ledyard. In due time, Ledyard reached St Petersburg, secured passports, and was within 200 miles of Kamchatka when he was forced to go into winter quarters. In the meantime the empress changed her mind, withdrew her permission, and Ledyard was arrested. The whole episode is significant for showing how formidable a trip overland from the United States to the Pacific Ocean must have appeared at the time.

In 1804, the president sent Meriwether Lewis and William Clark up the Missouri River beyond the Rocky Mountains and down the Columbia, until they reached the Pacific Ocean. They brought back an account of the Far West that lay beyond the West that Jefferson knew.

Lewis had parted from Jefferson at Washington, DC within a few days of the receipt of the news from Paris announcing the Louisiana Purchase. But it was not until May 1804 that his party of explorers left St Louis on their 8000-mile journey, which was to last two years and four months. One of the guides was the Shoshone woman Sacajawea, who provided great assistance in guiding them up the Missouri River and across the mountains to the Columbia River.

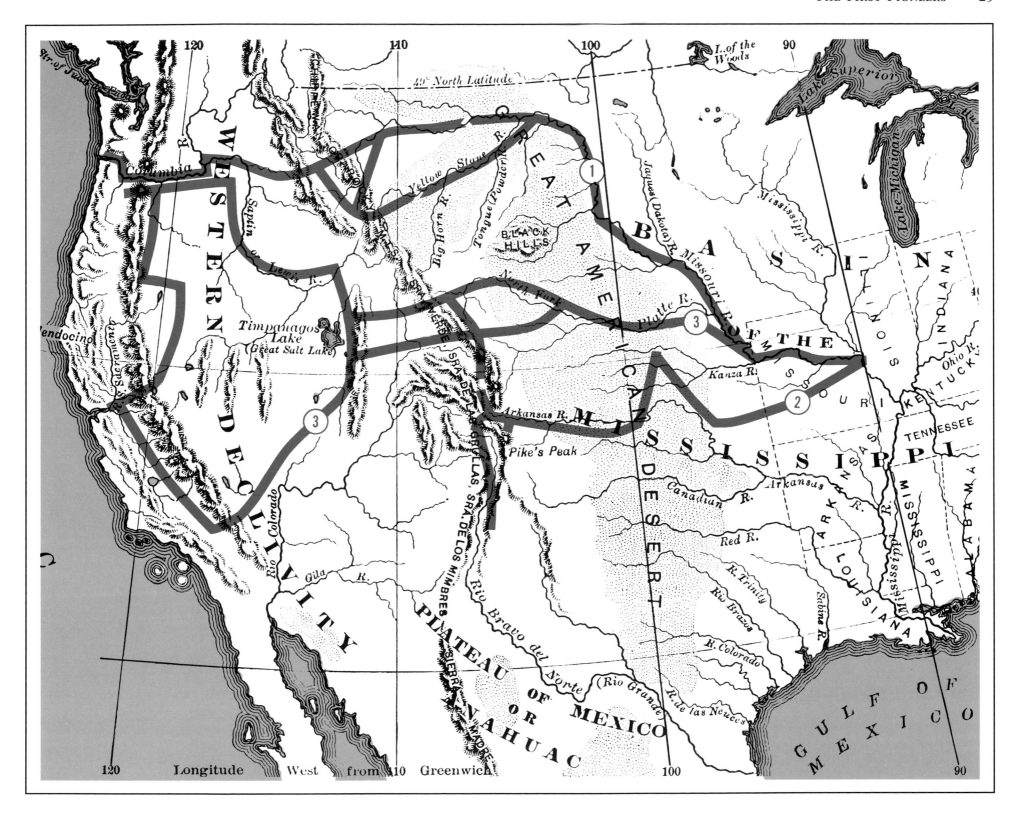

Right: Sacajawea, the famous Indian woman who guided Lewis and Clark through the Rocky Mountains to the Columbia River.

The expedition leaders had expected to have difficulties with hostile Indians, but they wrote in their journals that they 'experienced more difficulties from the navigation of the Missouri than dangers from the savages.' These dangers were due to the river's swift current, numerous snags, and caving banks, which threatened shipwreck to their frail canoes. Much of the time Lewis and Clark traveled on foot, hunting, collecting specimens and examining the countryside. As they later recalled, their greatest difficulties came from the 'trio of pests–mosquitoes, eye gnats and prickly pears–equal to any three curses that ever poor Egypt labored under.'

In the last week of October 1804, after ascending the Missouri River for 1600 miles, they reached a village of the Mandan Indians near the present site of the city of Bismarck, North Dakota and went into winter quarters. From there they sent back letters to President Jefferson, together with nine cages of living animals and birds, besides boxes containing specimens of rocks, plants and Indian dress. After five months at Fort Mandan, the expedition started out again. Clark wrote that he 'could not but esteem this moment of my departure as among the most happy of my life.' Passing the mouth of the Yellowstone, the party continued up the main river until they came to the Great Falls of the Missouri, a veil of spray 80 feet high descending between lofty cliffs of massive rock. From here, Sacajawea guided them through the Rocky Mountains to the Columbia River. The explorers camped by the mouth of the Columbia on 15 November 1805, and Captain Clark himself took Sacajawea and her husband to see the Pacific Ocean on 7 January 1806.

The party spent the winter of 1805-1806 on the Pacific Coast. They started back east in March 1806, and Sacajawea and her husband returned across the mountains with them to their Mandan village, where they were paid $500 for their services, a sum sufficient to build them a good cabin and buy many ponies.

When Lewis and Clark returned from their explorations in 1806, there were already other efforts under way to find out what it was that Jefferson had bought. During the previous winter, a young lieutenant in the army, Zebulon Montgomery Pike, had been sent up the Mississippi River from St Louis to ascertain the source of the great river. He did not find the source because the region was under thick ice and heavy snow, but he brought home much information about the country above the mouth of the Minnesota River. In the summer of 1806, Pike was sent out again, this time to find the sources of the Red River and the Arkansas. Again he found neither, but he saw the great peak which has come to be known as Pikes Peak, and he visited the park where the Rio Grande rises in southern Colorado. He was arrested by Spanish soldiers for trespassing in their territory, so nothing west of the Rio Grande could upon any claim be treated as a part of the Louisiana Purchase. He was escorted–half prisoner, half guest–through New Mexico, the northern part of Mexico, and Texas, and in 1807 he was returned unharmed to the US Army post at Natchitoches. His account of his travels, published soon after, fired the ambition of traders on the Missouri border to visit Santa Fe and capture the markets of the Spanish settlers.

In surveying the Spanish activities in the Great Plains region from 1528 to 1848–the end of the Spanish-Mexican regime–it becomes clear that the Spaniards enjoyed unusual success as explorers, but that they were notably unsuccessful as colonists. The Spanish failure to take and hold the Great Plains may be attributed in large measure to the nature of the problems found within the country, and not to the European situation. By 1600, the Spaniards had taken Mexico and had thrown their advance guard northward along the mountains as far as Santa Fe. On the east they were in

Facing page: An EO Beman photograph of the first camp of the John Wesley Powell expedition in the willows on the Green River, Wyoming Territory.

Above: **General John Fremont was the first to make a scientific survey of the Pacific Coast and to publicize his southwestern route to San Francisco.**

Florida. A century later they were in eastern Texas on the French Louisiana border. However, if a Spaniard wanted to go from San Antonio to Santa Fe, he did not make a direct journey across the Great Plains, but instead took the Camino Real, went south to Durango, then turned west and north and skirted the mountains until he came to Santa Fe. He went hundreds of miles out of the direct way, thus avoiding the open Plains country.

In 1821, when Spain lost her possessions, the situation had not changed. There were Spanish settlements on both sides of the Plains, but none *on* the Plains. For 27 more years (1821-1848) Mexico exercised nominal jurisdiction over the region without altering the status left by Spain. The result is that there exist on the Great Plains today but few reminders of Spanish ownership. Here and there a place name of creeks, lakes and hills, but nothing more.

It is apparent that the Spaniards avoided the Great Plains, or failed there, for two reasons, both fairly independent of European politics. In the first place, the country itself did not attract them; in the second place, the Plains Indians repelled whatever efforts they did make at travel, occupation or residence in the region. The result was that the Spaniards never did more than nibble around the margins of the Great Plains.

While the Spaniards were experimenting with their frontier system on the southern margin of the Great Plains, the Anglo-Americans of the United States were approaching the region from the east, and about the time the Spaniards were ready to confess the failure of their efforts, the Americans were just beginning theirs. By the first two decades of the nineteenth century, people were coming slowly but persistently through the forests east of the Mississippi, felling trees, building cabins, making rail fences, digging shallow wells or drinking from the numerous springs and perennial streams, advancing shoulder to shoulder and pushing the Native Americans westward toward the Plains. In the first half of the nineteenth century, the advance guard of this moving host of forest homemakers emerged into a new environment, where there were no forests, no logs for cabins, no rails for fences and few springs and running streams. Instead, before them lay a wide land inhabited by Indians. Beyond the Mississippi was the natural barrier of the Great Plains. The pioneers threw themselves upon it, armed and equipped with the weapons, tools, ideas and institutions which had served them so long and so well in the woods that now lay behind them. Inevitably they failed in their first efforts, and they continued to fail until they worked out a technique of pioneering adapted to the Plains rather than to the woodland. The official records of many of these trips—to say nothing of journals, memoirs and special studies—are readily available. The objective of most of these exploring parties was the Pacific Coast or the Rocky Mountains.

Lewis and Clark led the first official exploring party across the Plains. But before Lewis and Clark returned from their trip across the northern Plains, Zebulon Pike had set out to cross the middle Plains to the Rocky Mountains.

At the same time in the North, considerable trade was already being conducted in beaver pelts. This enterprise was dominated by Manuel Lisa, a Spaniard, and by the Frenchmen Auguste and Pierre Chouteau, and was conducted mainly along the upper Missouri. From here, the trappers pushed out in every direction where beaver ground might be discovered. It was these trappers who first explored the wilderness, but they seldom put anything on record.

In 1811, Henry, one of Lisa's company, built a trading post at the head of the Snake River, and larger operators gradually stepped into the fur business. Before the sale of

Left: Rounding Windy Point during a climb of Pikes Peak in Colorado in the winter of 1890.

Louisiana, the French had virtually dominated the fur industry in what is now the United States. From New Orleans they had worked up the river to St Louis, and from St Louis they reached out towards the Rocky Mountains, inducing the Indians to bring in furs, and sending out trappers to collect them. They also had come from Quebec and Montreal and from the shores of Hudson Bay. They knew every detail of the land long before any surveyor arrived to map it.

When Louisiana became part of the United States, Congress tried to drive out the foreign trappers, particularly those of the British Hudson Bay Company, in order to protect the traffic for American advantage.

John Jacob Astor, a New York merchant, took a lead in organizing American fur companies. Stockaded posts were built for agency houses to trade with Indians. Each year the goods for the Indians were sent to the posts: blankets, guns, powder, tools, needles, beads and all the trinkets the Indians lacked and wanted.

In 1810, John Jacob Astor organized the Pacific Fur Company, and the next year a party arrived by sea to erect a fort at the mouth of the Columbia, across from the site of present-day Astoria, Oregon. The British Northwest Company did all they could to inhibit the Pacific Fur Company from building or trading, but nevertheless the fort *was* completed and the company began its operations.

From 1812 until 1846, the fur trade was to be the chief resource of the Far West. During the War of 1812, Astoria was taken by the British but it was restored to the owners at the conclusion of peace, despite the British contending that it was simply a restoration of private property that had encroached on British territory, and had no bearing on the American claim of ownership to Oregon. The treaty of Ghent called for a return of 'all territory, places and possessions whatsoever,' except some specified on the Atlantic Coast. No agreement on a boundary could be reached, so the United States adhered to its claim on the whole Oregon country on the basis of purchase, discovery, exploration and settlement.

The third *official* American expedition across the Plains was that of Stephen H Long in 1819-1820. As originally planned, it was known as the Yellowstone Expedition, designed to ascend the Missouri River for the purpose of establishing military posts to protect the fur trade and to counteract the influence of the British in the northern region. The public looked upon the expedition as the initiation of an extensive development of the trans-Mississippi region by the federal government.

The three pioneer expeditions served to acquaint the American public with the character of that part of the Great Plains between the Missouri River and the Rocky Mountains. The explorers had followed the principal rivers–the Missouri, the Arkansas, the Platte and the Canadian–and had made fairly accurate records of the vegetable and animal life of the region, along with some more or less valuable information about the indigenous people. They had marked out in a measure the trails that were to be thrown across the Plains to Oregon, California and Santa Fe. Long had prepared a map on which he included the Great American Desert, and thus the desert nature of this vast region became a reality in the American mind.

Right: This map of the territory west of the Rocky Mountains and between Monterey Bay and Puget Sound was drawn in 1837 after the expeditions of Benjamin Louis Eulalie de Bonneville (1796-1878). A French-born American citizen, Bonneville explored much of the Great Basin country. He helped to confirm that Lake Timpanagos was a single lake *(compare to map on page 9)* and he renamed it for himself. It is now known as the Great Salt Lake, but the adjacent salt flats still bear Bonneville's name.

The map includes the Columbia River, the legendary 'River of the West' *(see map on page 23).* Its mouth was discovered by Martin d'Aguilar in 1603, but the sandbar at its mouth was so treacherous that the river was never explored until after the American seaman Robert Gray found a way to navigate it in 1792. His ship was called *Columbia,* hence the present name of the West's broadest river.

Bonneville always included a few personal touches on his maps, including the place west of the lake where he 'killed 25 Indians.'

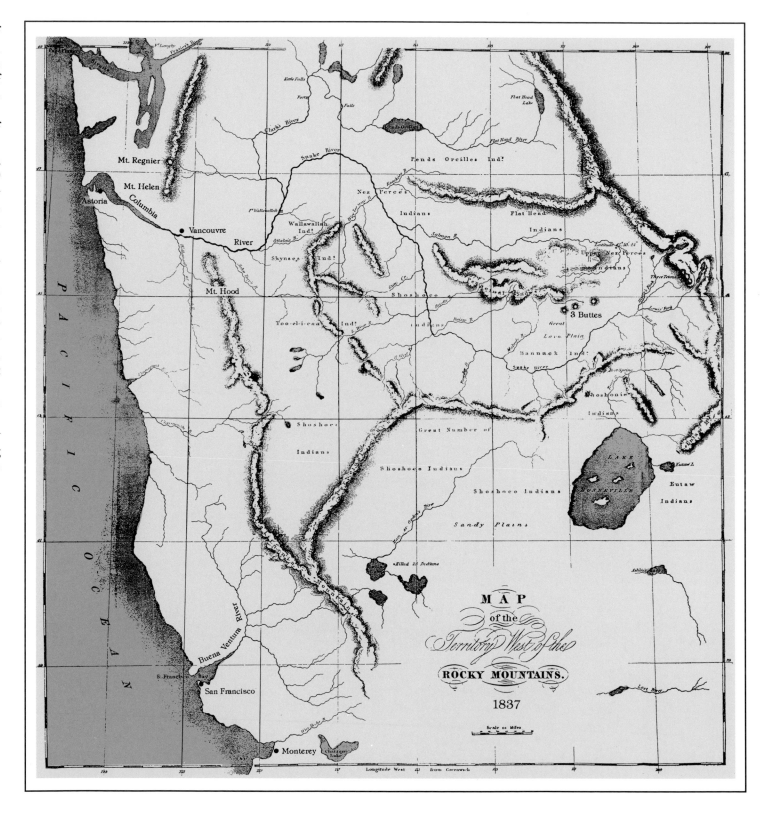

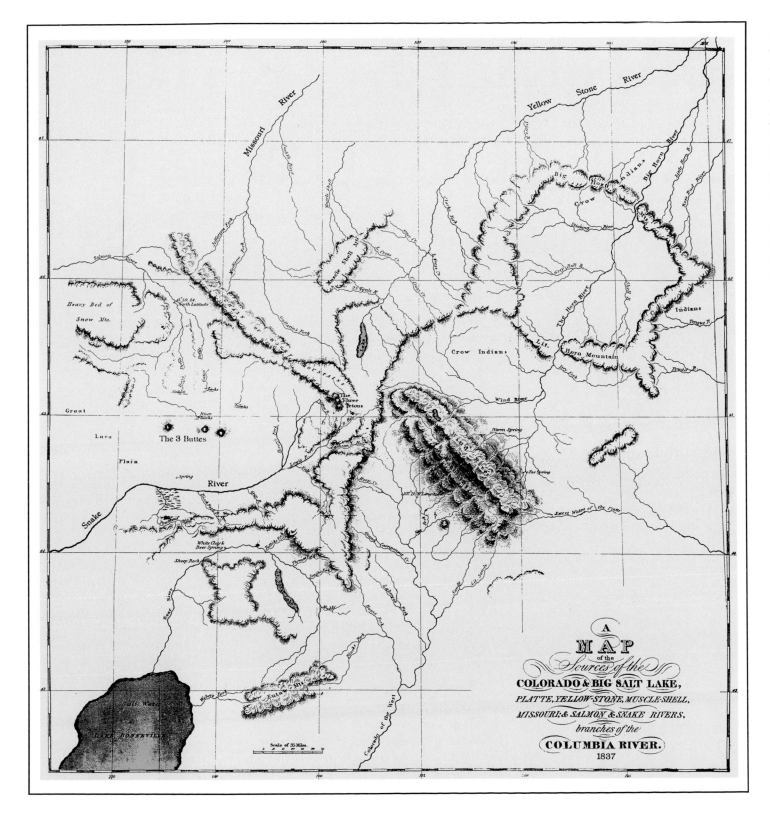

A MAP
of the
Sources of the
COLORADO & BIG SALT LAKE,
PLATTE, YELLOW-STONE, MUSCLE-SHELL,
MISSOURI; & SALMON & SNAKE RIVERS,
branches of the
COLUMBIA RIVER.
1837

Left: This map, dating from 1837, covers the area between what are now northern Utah and south central Montana. It shows Benjamin Louis Bonneville's attempts to locate the sources of the Columbia, Colorado, Platte, Yellowstone, Musselshell, Missouri, Salmon and Snake rivers. In those days 'Yellowstone' was written as two words, but Bonneville's calligrapher simply misspelled 'Musselshell.'

As usual, Bonneville indicated areas where he made contact with native peoples. He also pinpointed the location of springs and sinks, facts that would be of use to future travellers.

The Santa Fe Trail and the Southwest

Above: The Palace of the Governors in Santa Fe, New Mexico dates to the seventeenth century.

The great Santa Fe Trail ran southwest from the bend of the Missouri River across the plains to New Mexico. Although it was first used soon after Zebulon Pike's expedition in 1807, regular use of the trail began after Mexican independence in 1821, with the wagons crossing the Kansas plains to the great bend of the Arkansas River. The main routes ascended near La Junta in Colorado, across Raton Pass and down the slopes from the north to the city of Santa Fe.

There was a short cut, dry and dangerous, that crossed the Arkansas near the Mexican border which went through the Cimarroji River country, entering Santa Fe from the east. Important as it was, the Santa Fe Trail–and its extension to California, the Spanish Trail–was not an emigrant road. It was used chiefly by traders, whose prairie schooners full of goods raced across the plains and followed the market down the Rio Grande, sometimes crossing the Chihuahua desert below El Paso and penetrating as far south as to Mexico City itself.

California Alta (the present state of California as opposed to Baja California, which is still part of Mexico), was definitely claimed by the Spaniards, at least as far as Cape Mendocino. However, it was not until 1769 that Captain Portola and Padre Junipero (Miguel Jose) Serra were sent from Baja California to establish settlements in the form of missions in this Far North. The first footing was at San Diego. From that point mission after mission was founded, the Native Americans brought to prayer and song–albeit by the lash and sword to a great extent–and the most unique era in the history of California began. Eighteen mission settlements were in operation before the beginning of the nineteenth century, while three others were constructed later. Gardens, vineyards, acres of grain fields, and thousands of head of sheep, cattle and horses surrounded each settlement, and the wonderful fertility of the California soil was quickly demonstrated.

There was no road between these missions and those of New Mexico. In order to find one, Franciscan priests Padre Escalante and Padre Dominguez left Santa Fe on 29 July 1776 for Monterey. They proceeded northward into what is now the state of Colorado, possibly with the intention of passing the great barrier of the canyons of the

Above: An ox train on the Santa Fe Trail
in the nineteenth century.

Above: **Fred Loring with his mule *Evil Merodach* in 1871. Timothy O'Sullivan took this photograph about 48 hours before Loring was brutally murdered by Apache-Mohaves while en route by stage from Prescott in Arizona Territory to San Bernadino, California. Loring had been with the Wheeler expedition as general assistant and correspondent and was returning to the East.**

Colorado River at the crossing afterwards named for Captain Gunnison, the same point where the 'Spanish Trail' was established in 1830 by the American William Wolfskill. They had heard of Salt Lake but did not go there. Instead they turned south and traveled along the western flanks of the Wasatch.

Santa Fe, as we have noted, was simply very difficult to approach from the rest of the Spanish North American territories. However, by 1800 Santa Fe had developed considerably and had a population of more than 4000, while in the surrounding valleys thousands of Spaniards, Mexicans and Puebloans were cultivating crops mainly by irrigation and herding large flocks of sheep and herds of cattle and horses. They sorely needed manufactured goods and suddenly, the likely source was the United States.

The road to Mexico was long and difficult and duties were high. Several Americans, discovering this situation, inaugurated some small but profitable trading operations as early as 1802. The New Mexican people welcomed the Yankee traders because they could satisfy their wants. The governor, who was also the government, welcomed them because he grew rich on taxes. Thus trade increased rapidly. This was the beginning of the Santa Fe Trail.

It is probable that the American migrations to Oregon and to California would have produced an Americanization of the latter even had there not been a war with Mexico. As it turned out, however, war hastened the process. When in 1846 preparations were made to invade Mexico, an army was assembled on the border, mobilized at Fort Leavenworth (which had been built in 1827 to protect the Santa Fe trade) and marched into New Mexico under the command of Stephen Watts Kearny. From New Mexico, Kearny, guided by Christopher 'Kit' Carson, proceeded to California. When he arrived at Los Angeles, he found California already largely conquered by the joint work of the Navy and of resident United States citizens, the latter headed by John C Fremont.

The Santa Fe Trail originated at Council Grove, a place whose name indicated a pleasant contrast to the hot expanse of the shadeless Plains. The Santa Fe traders here elected a captain of the caravan, whose powers were undefined and vague. His business was to direct the order of travel, to select the camping sites and to exercise such authority as his natural powers of leadership and the democratic disposition of his followers would permit. A party of 100 wagons would be divided into four sections, with a lieutenant over each section. Tourists and hangers-on were welcomed in order to give added strength to the party, though every man in the caravan was required by the 'common law of the prairies' to stand guard duty in his turn. When the party had crossed the dangerous Plains country and come within 140 miles of Santa Fe, the wagon train was disbanded, and men who on the Plains had bound themselves together for mutual protection against a common enemy again became commercial rivals.

The Santa Fe trade rapidly developed. In 1824, Augustus Storrs made his report to Senator Benton Thomas Hart, and that indefatigable legislator introduced a bill for a survey of the route, which was conducted in 1825-1826 by JC Brown. The work was done by chain and compass and corrected by latitude and longitude observations. In 1824, wagons, to some extent, took the place of pack animal trains, and after that the wagons predominated. Thousands of tons of merchandise were transported over the 775 miles of this dangerous road that began from Westport (the present Kansas City), Independence and Franklin.

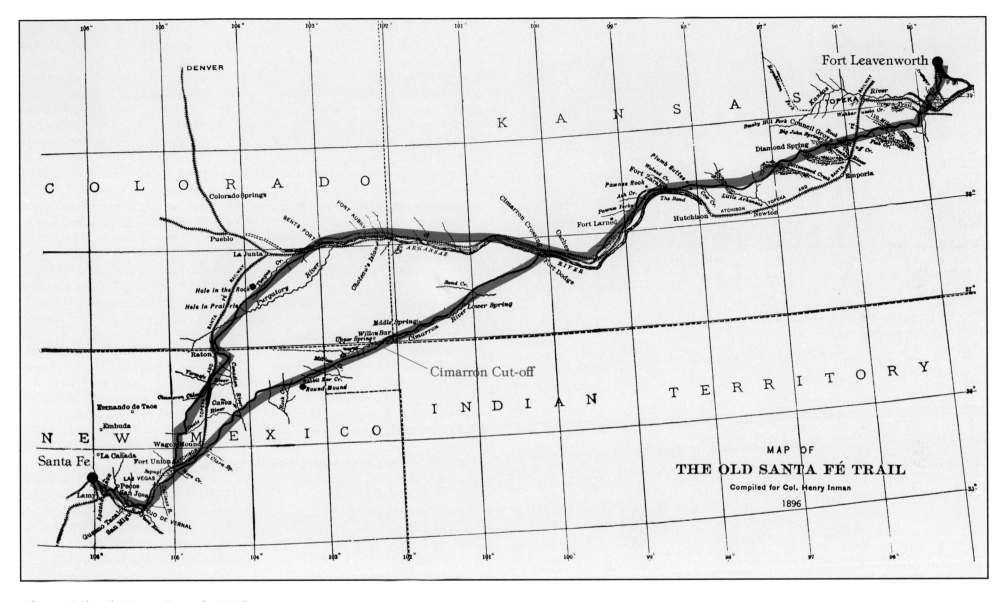

Above: Colonel Henry Inman's 1896 map shows the evolution of a trail that had been in service for nearly a century. Santa Fe itself dates from 1609. The Cimarron Cut-off, which was essentially a short cut, was also a much more dangerous trail than the main Santa Fe Trail. The Atchison, Topeka & Santa Fe Railroad generally followed the original trail and was completed into Santa Fe in 1880.

Above: **Jim Bridger was the archetypical mountain man and a legendary western scout.**

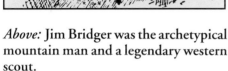

Right: **Kit Carson, the famed hunter, trapper, guide and military scout, accompanied Fremont on his explorations of the West in 1842.**

Facing page: **D Griffiths photographed this man with wagon parts and equipment on the muddy floor of Canyon de Chelly in the Navajo Reservation in Arizona Territory in 1903.**

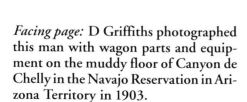

These were also the starting places used by numerous trappers and fur traders, who were exceedingly skillful and capable. Some became famous, like Jim Bridger and Kit Carson, while others of as great or greater accomplishments–like Jedediah Smith–are less well known. Thomas L 'Peg-leg' Smith, (so called because of a wooden leg he wore after the loss of a leg due to an arrow shot), was occupied largely as a horse thief. He operated between the various native tribes, commonly joining the raid of one tribe or another as suited his plans, but his greatest hauls were made in California. He would send spies ahead, and then at the given hour would sweep through the country driving the horses before him.

General William H Ashley, one of the most distinguished of the traders, came to the mountains in 1824 and took a wheeled cannon through South Pass in 1827. Wagons were first pulled through this pass by Captain Bonneville in 1832. Bonneville, on leave of absence from the Army, lived the life of a fur trader and enjoyed it so much that he neglected to return home, or even to send word of his intentions, when his leave was up. He visited Salt Lake and planned for its exploration but Walker, who was to do the work, went instead on across, by way of the Humboldt, to California.

The discovery of the Great Salt Lake is awarded to Jim Bridger, though it has been said that Etienne Provost was there in 1820, four years earlier. Several trappers circumnavigated it in search of beaver streams in 1826. Bonneville attempted to carry his operations into the Oregon region, but the hostility of the Hudson Bay Company compelled him to desist, as it had every other American. The Californians were also opposed to American trappers, and they instigated attacks by Indians against them. The officials of New Mexico imposed on American trappers and traders, and, as in California, they were frequently thrown into prison, where they were badly treated.

In 1837, when Texas achieved its independence, the matter of placing the boundary at the Rio Grande had not been settled, but New Mexico was dissatisfied with conditions and would be glad to join Texas against the Mexican government, which was simply the barbarous governor, Armijo. Accordingly, the Santa Fe expedition was organized in 1841. It was largely a commercial venture, but it had a powerful guard.

The conquest was expected to be accomplished pleasantly and briefly, but the expedition, not knowing the way, arrived in the Rio Grande valley in a separated and demoralized condition. Deception then gave Armijo the upper hand. Some of the Texans were slaughtered and the rest captured. California during this time was receiving settlers from the United States, and a trade similar to the Santa Fe had grown to considerable proportions, but it was conducted by sea. The Mexican government was disturbed.

The Californians had affiliated themselves with foreigners and were highly independent. So in 1836, the following resolution was passed by a newly formed state, of which JB Alvarado was made civil governor: 'The said California shall be erected into a free and governing state, establishing a congress which shall dictate all the particulars of the country and elect the other supreme powers necessary.'

About this time, a Eugene Duflot de Mofras, a Frenchman traveling in Alta California, wrote: 'England and the United States flatter themselves alike with the idea of taking California from Mexico. It is, moreover, evident to us that California will belong to whatever nation chooses to send there a man-of-war and 200 men.' In other words, the first nation to make an aggressive move would be the one which would gain the prize of California. However, while Great Britain and the United States had no intention of becoming involved in a war over this question, war with Mexico

Above: The multicolored canyons of the Colorado badlands are as spectacular a sight today as they were in the 1800s.

Facing page: Stanton G Smith photographed this rider as he filled his keg from a desert well 30 miles north of Palomas in Arizona Territory. His horse refreshes himself nearby.

was expected. Texas and Mexico were nominally at war, so it required only the annexation of Texas to the United States–a move already being urged in Congress–to bring about war against Mexico.

The dividing line between the East and the West cuts the state of Texas into two almost equal parts. In 1821, Stephen F Austin led a group of immigrants from the United States into Texas, which was then a Mexican province. However, he did not attempt to make his settlement near the Plains portion of the state, but chose that portion of the state which is similar to the more fertile regions of the Mississippi Valley. Like the people who two decades later went to Oregon, he sought the timbered and well-watered environment, along the Brazos and Colorado rivers, in which the settlers he expected to introduce would feel at home.

Austin understood the Indian situation in Texas. In eastern Texas were the generally peaceful Cherokees, Choctaws and Caddos. Among the settlers were the Tonkawas, and below them on the coast were the ferocious but numerically weak Karankawas. To the west were the Wacos and Tahuacanos.

In the summer of 1826, after several years of skirmishes with the Plains Indians, Austin called together the representatives of the various militia districts to adopt a plan by which to guard against the incursions of the Indians. The result of this conference was an arrangement to keep from 20 to 30 mounted rangers in service all the time. Austin had responded to the problem by organizing the Texas Rangers, which later developed into a mounted fighting organization whose reputation became legendary.

Just as the explorers who set out from Missouri to cross the Plains had to leave their boats and take to wagons and horses, so the Texans found it necessary to mount their horses in order to meet the mounted Plains Indians. The Texans still had to learn much about horses and horseback fighting, but they had no choice in the matter if they were to succeed in their contest with the Indians for possession of the Plains.

From 1821 to 1836, these venturesome Texans were the outriders of the American frontier. They could not go northwest, west, or southwest without coming into the range of the Comanches and other mounted Indians. They were also in contact with the Mexicans–not so much with the Mexican population as with the Mexican government, under which they had voluntarily placed themselves but with which they never found themselves in complete accord.

Potentially, Texas was a center of three conflicting civilizations–that of the Mexicans, the Texans and the Plains Indians. The potential conflict soon became a real one, eventuating in that tempestuous period beginning with the Texas revolution and ending with the Mexican War, between which events the Texans maintained an independent republic.

During the 10 years of the republic, Texans had no peace. Mexico refused to recognize the independence of its lost province and maintained a constant threat of war, which expressed itself in raids into Texas, during which San Antonio was twice captured by Mexican armies.

The Texans also made two attacks against Mexico. In 1841, the Santa Fe expedition left Austin with the ostensible purpose of establishing the jurisdiction of Texas over Santa Fe and, if possible, of making good the claim of Texas to the upper Rio Grande valley. In 1842, a party of Texans set out to invade Mexico. Their disastrous venture is known as the Mier expedition, because when the Texans reached Mier they were captured by a Mexican army. Both the Santa Fe and the Mier expeditions ended in disaster, with most of the participants being captured and some executed.

Above: A Texas cowboy and his fast mount. Note his Colt six-shooter at the ready.

Opposite: Riflemen on the plains dismount to pose for the photographer, circa 1883.

From their long experience with both Mexicans and Indians, the Texans learned that they could never afford to surrender. The memory of the massacre at the Alamo in 1836 affected the attitude of all those who found themselves in conflict with the Mexicans.

The Texas border war was not a warfare of pitched battles, but of great distances, sudden incursions, and rapid flight on horseback. Attackers always came on horseback, with an organization that was mobile, fleet and elusive. They had to be met and pursued on horseback with an organization equally mobile. From these hard conditions evolved the organization of the Texas Rangers. Stationed in the frontier town of San Antonio under the leadership of Captain John Coffee Hays of Tennessee, they scoured the border in search of marauding Indians and pillaging Mexicans. What these men had brought with them to the West was blended with what they acquired after their arrival in Texas into a type of man that could 'ride like a Mexican, trail like an Indian, shoot like a Tennesseean and fight like a devil!'

The Texas Rangers became one of the most engaging icons of the American West. So did the weapon that they adopted as their own: the six-shot revolver known as the

'six-shooter.' Samuel Colt first began marketing his revolvers in the 1830s, and by 1845, it had become the standard weapon of the Texas Rangers.

The weapons used by the Rangers had to be suited to mounted combat. The arms originally carried by the Rangers were the same as those used by the American pioneers east of the Mississippi, the American long rifle, a weapon which has been designated as one of the principal factors in the conquest of America. However, this rifle was designed for use on the ground, not on horseback. It was developed in the woods for service when the user had both feet planted firmly on solid earth.

The 'hair trigger,' the 'double sights,' the 'fine bead,' are terms significant of a weapon nicely adjusted that needs to be carefully aimed. In the decade between 1830 and 1840, the cap-and-ball rifle was still in use, the loading of which was a meticulous and time-consuming task. Its powder had to be measured and poured, the ball rammed down the barrel with a long rod, the tube must be 'primed' and the cap or flint adjusted.

All this took about a minute, and in a fight, much can happen in a minute. The rifle was no horseman's weapon.

The sword and lance, the horseman's traditional weapons, were outworn relics of the pre-gunpowder era. The Mexicans used the lance, as did the Plains Indians, but the Texans never used either. Once, when there was talk of equipping the Texas Rangers with swords, an old Texan remarked, 'They would doubtless be of great service to the Rangers, especially in snake country.'

The Comanche warrior carried a 14-foot spear, a plain or sinew-backed bow, and a quiver of arrows tipped with flint or steel. These he used effectively on both game and enemy. With pistols that existed prior to the advent of the revolver, the Texans carried at most three shots, while the Comanche carried 20 or more arrows. If it took a Texan a minute to reload his weapon, an Indian could in that time ride 300 yards and discharge all 20 of his arrows. The Texan had to dismount in order to use his rifle effectively, but the Indian could remain mounted throughout the combat. Apparently the one advantage possessed by the gunman was a weapon of longer range and more accuracy than an Indian bow. However, the agility of an Indian and the rapidity of his movements did much to offset this advantage. The marvelous marksmanship of earlier days was due to the fact that the first shot was frequently the only shot.

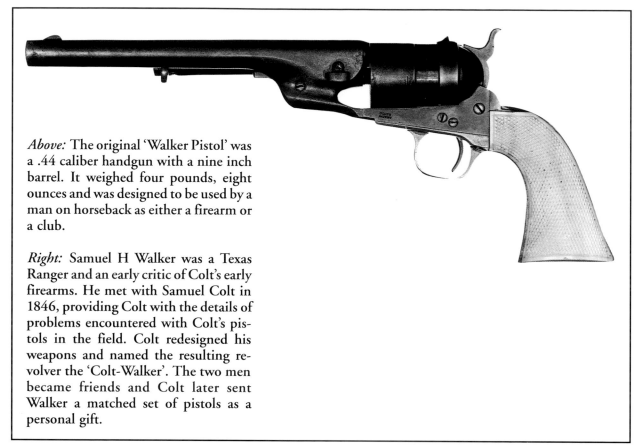

Above: The original 'Walker Pistol' was a .44 caliber handgun with a nine inch barrel. It weighed four pounds, eight ounces and was designed to be used by a man on horseback as either a firearm or a club.

Right: Samuel H Walker was a Texas Ranger and an early critic of Colt's early firearms. He met with Samuel Colt in 1846, providing Colt with the details of problems encountered with Colt's pistols in the field. Colt redesigned his weapons and named the resulting revolver the 'Colt-Walker'. The two men became friends and Colt later sent Walker a matched set of pistols as a personal gift.

Undoubtedly, the Texans needed a new weapon, something with a reserve power and capable of 'continuous' action–a weapon more rapid than the Indians' arrows, of longer reach than his spear and, above all, one adapted to use on horseback. The man who supplied the weapon that fulfilled all these necessities was a Connecticut Yankee, Samuel Colt. In 1835–the same year the Texan revolt began–Colt took out his first patent in England. In 1863, he took out a patent in America, the same year the Texans established their independence from Mexico as the Republic of Texas. By 1838, a company had been organized at Paterson, New Jersey to manufacture Colt's patented firearms.

The close relationship of Texas and the Rangers to the evolution of this distinctive American weapon is exemplified in the very names given to these early revolvers. The first model which became famous was called the 'Texas.' A second model, which had certain improvements over the old, was brought out around 1842. It was a Texas Ranger who suggested the improvements, and it was for him that the improved weapon was named. This man, Samuel H Walker, then captain of the Rangers, had been sent to New York to purchase a supply of the latest firearms, and while there he arranged to meet Colt.

The result of several days of very friendly conference between Walker and Colt was a new type of pistol–the first military revolver. Walker suggested that, while the Texas was a wonderful weapon, it was too light; that, as it was in three pieces while being loaded, a mounted man was very liable to lose a part. A trigger guard was necessary so that the strength and weight of the pistol would be such as to render it serviceable as a club when empty. The pistol which Colt produced to meet these requirements was named the 'Walker Pistol.' The 'Texas,' 'Walker' and the term 'six-shooter,' all coined by the Rangers, bear evidence to the fact that the 'Lone Star Republic' had much to do with the development of the new weapon.

The exact date which the revolvers were brought to Texas remains uncertain, but a copy of a signed statement by two Rangers dates their appearance in Texas in 1839. The following year, John C Hays and his men were stationed in San Antonio, and it was Hays and his men, Walker among them, who proved conclusively the value of the revolvers. Years later, a Comanche chief who had fought against the Rangers said that he never wanted to fight Jack Hays and his Rangers again, that they had a shot for every finger on the hand, and that he lost half his warriors, who died for a hundred miles along the trail toward Devil's River.

In 1850, Major George T Howard of the old Texas army and Captain IS Sutton of the Rangers wrote the following testimonial to the effectiveness of the revolvers: 'They are the only weapon which enabled the experienced frontiersmen to defeat the mounted Indian in his own peculiar mode of warfare. ... We state, and with entire assurance of the fact, that the six-shooter is the arm which has rendered the name of Texas Ranger a check and terror to the bands of our frontier Indians.'

BY CONSENT OF THE MAYOR,

AN EXHIBITION OF

COLT'S PATENT

Repeating Rifles

Will be made at the Battery.

On Monday afternoon, 19th inst.

At half past 4 o'clock.

The public are respectfully invited to attend.   The instrument may also be examined at the store of Dick & Holmes, Vendue Range, who have a few of them for sale, price $150 each.

SAMUEL COLT, Patentee.

These Rifles are eight times more effective, and very little more expensive than the ordinary Rifle of equal finish.

DICK & HOLMES, Agents.

February 17th, 1838.

Above: Samuel Colt, founder of Colt's Patented Firearms. Colt's innovations included mass production techniques.

Shown *above right* is a Colt Walker Revolver, circa 1847. Samuel Colt also produced and exhibited rifles *(right)*.

Above: C Fly photographed the Orient Saloon at Bisbee, Arizona in 1900. We see a faro game in full blast. *Left to right* the players included Tony Downs, part owner; Doyle, a concert hall singer; a dealer named Johnny Murphy; and Smiley Lewis *(in silk hat)*. *Behind, standing* are Dutch Kid; Sleepy Dick, the porter; and Charlie Bassett *(with felt hat in the rear)*.

Facing page: A DH Payne photo of the rebuilding of Monument 40 along the Mexican border west of the Rio Grande. The 1892-1894 project was under the direction of the United States section of the International Boundary Commission.

Above: The lunchtime camp of a surveying outfit in the southwest part of Jornada Range Reserve in New Mexico on 17 October 1912.

Facing page: Neil M Judd photographed this discovery party and horses on the hot, slick rocks west of Navajo Mountain on their way to Rainbow Bridge in Utah in 1909.

89608

Facing page: Children in their Sunday clothes were captured on a photographic plate by AM Neal on 13 May 1908 standing in front of an adobe church in the Alamo National Forest in New Mexico Territory, now known as the Lincoln National Forest.

Above: A family poses with their dog and young children outside their log cabin in New Mexico Territory.

Facing page: This Arizona poker party was captured on a photographic plate by FA Ames in 1887 at John Doyle's ranch. Doyle, Judge Brown and Professor Burrison are seen at play.

Left: After the game, Brown, Burrison and Doyle picked up their rifles and did a little target shooting.

THE OREGON TRAIL AND THE NORTHWEST

Above: Wagons on the Oregon Trail. When they stopped for the night, the wagons were circled to provide mutual protection from Indian attacks.

Facing page: CE Watkins' 1867 photo of the boat terminal and train on the portage railroad on the Washington side of the Columbia River. The block house where railroad workers sought safety from Indian attacks is seen on the hill in the upper left.

The Oregon Trail began, where most of the trails began, at that stretch of the Missouri River where the river, after flowing southeast across the Dakotas, turns south along the western boundaries of Iowa and Missouri and then turns sharply eastward at the mouth of the Kansas River, eventually flowing into the Mississippi near St Louis. Eastern roads crossed the Missouri River at many places above the mouth of the Kansas, but the bend of the river at this point became known as 'the great bend,' or the mouth of the Missouri, and was the starting point for traders, soldiers, explorers and emigrants bound west. The Oregon Trail was the route of the emigration of 1843, and was most famous of all the routes. Francis Parkman, the great historian, traveled it while it was new and described it in his book *The Oregon Trail.*

In retrospect, the trail was more than a personal adventure for hearty pioneers. It was, by the 1840s, an instrument of national policy. By 1841, five years before the Mexican War, the United States had undisputed claim to less than one-half the territory west of the Mississippi. But at the same time, the winds of change were blowing for the colonial proprietorship of the other half. Great Britain held but a shaky grip on Oregon; Mexico saw California Alta tugging at its moorings, with New Mexico in much the same condition. Texas was already steering with her own crew by 1837. Russia had an uncertain foot on California at Rossiya (Fort Ross) and Bodega Bay.

Each year in May, when prairie grass was soft and prairie roads were dry enough to carry loads, the overland emigrants gathered along the Missouri above the bend, completing their outfits at the stores near Independence, Missouri. The emigrants were mainly dependent upon notes made from information gained from trappers and the very rough map which had been constructed to aid in the translation of the notes. It was very much like Columbus turning the prow of his vessel toward the center of limitless ocean, trusting to God and his own courage and genius for the discovery of a route and the ability to overcome difficulties. Likewise, the emigrants made every provision to meet emergencies that could be foreseen, but it was the vast unknown which might furnish insurmountable obstacles. In both cases, there was indomitable courage.

Above: The covered wagons of the pioneers offered little protection from Indian attacks on the open plains.

Facing page: The states and territories of the American West as they appeared in 1889, just prior to the division of Dakota Territory into the states of North Dakota and South Dakota. Indian Territory would be cut in half to create Oklahoma Territory, then disappear entirely, when this area became the state of Oklahoma in 1907. Arizona and New Mexico would remain as territories until 1912.

The shaded vertical line marks the border between the East and the American West.

The main routes for the opening of the American West are shown. The oldest was the Santa Fe Trail (1), which is shown in more detail in the map on page 35. The great Overland Trail (2) began at points between Independence, Missouri and Omaha, Nebraska and crossed the Nebraska prairies following the Platte. It forked to form the Bozeman Trail (3) into Montana and the Mormon Trail (6) into Utah, but the main route became the Oregon Trail (4), which had the greatest number of travellers in the early years. Technically, it went all the way to the Pacific at Astoria, but most travellers spilled into the Willamette Valley south of Portland.

With the California gold rush of 1849, however, the California Trail (5) became the most important of the great forks of the Overland Trail.

The covered wagons, or 'prairie schooners,' these pioneers used were much like the heavy wagons built by the Pennsylvania Dutch in Conestoga country on the Susquehanna, which were known as 'Conestoga' or 'Pittsburgh' wagons. Their heavy wheels carried great wooden bodies, and these were covered with canvas tops supported on bows of bent white oak. Drawn by horses or oxen, with families walking alongside driving cattle and other livestock, the wagons made up caravans that crawled along the trail. At dusk, the captain of the caravan (for the emigrants organized under a captain for safety from Indian attacks), directed the wagons into a circular corral, an enclosure into which the cattle were driven for the night and from which they could be neither stampeded nor stolen.

The first concern of the emigrants was the construction of wagons for the trip West. There were neither boats nor ferrymen on the route, so the wagons had to be made strong with beds so jointed that they were watertight, and thus could serve as boats when crossing rivers. The covers were made of tent cloth, which had to be impervious to rain. The wagons were all constructed as the skill, workmanship and material permitted. They were drawn by four yoke of cattle each, with two cows for each wagon that had been broken to work in a yoke, so that the emigrants would have fresh milk available on their journey. Provision was also made for a supply of butter. A churn was fastened to the outside of each wagon, into which surplus milk was poured. The violent shaking it would receive in passing over rough roads would produce excellent butter.

Every other article, which experience had taught them would be required, was also procured. Fresh meat would be available en route, as the whole country through which they were to travel was alive with all kinds of game, especially buffalo, elk, deer and antelope.

By 1846, although a considerable number of adventurous Americans had already crossed the plains, there still was no road between the Missouri River and Pacific Ocean, which deserved any better appellation than 'trail.' The Oregon Trail, well trodden by this time, left Westport Landing, or Independence, at the mouth of the Kansas, and ran across the country to the Platte River, at the head of Grand Island and Fort Kearney. The main Oregon Trail followed the south bank of the Platte to the junction of the North and South forks, and then followed the south bank of the North Platte through Mitchell Pass to Fort Laramie.

The Mormons, who crossed the Platte in 1847, followed the north bank, which was thereafter know as the Mormon Trail. Both trails merged as one along the Sweetwater branch of the North Platte, and beyond the head of the Sweetwater the wagons crossed the Continental Divide through South Pass, which had been first visited by fur traders about 1823.

West of South Pass, the Oregon Trail followed the Snake River, passing Fort Hall. It then continued to Oregon, where the Snake and Columbia merge near Walla Walla, Washington. From here, it continued through the Columbia Gorge to the mouth of the Willamette River at Fort Vancouver (now Vancouver, Washington) near present-day Portland. Although it technically continued to the Pacific Ocean at Astoria (across the Columbia from Lewis and Clark's 1805 camp), the practical objective was the rich Willamette Valley south of the Columbia.

The trail was bordered with many graves of those who died on the way and with goods discarded from wagons as animals became too worn out to draw heavy loads. There were broken wagons, abandoned where they fell apart, and the skeletons of

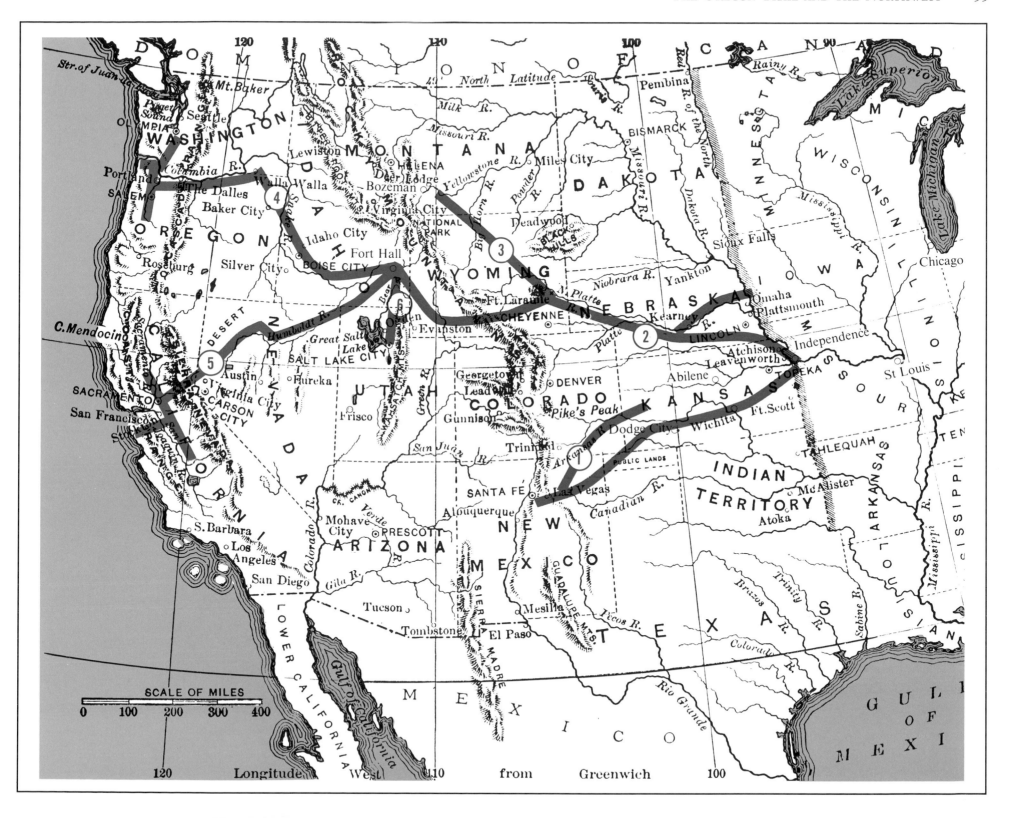

horses and oxen, picked clean by coyotes that howled around the campfires every night and scavenged campgrounds after the travelers pulled out. It has been estimated that each mile of the 2000-mile journey cost 17 lives–a total of 34,000.

By 1848, thanks to the trail, Congress made Oregon a territory. The Oregon migration, well developed by 1843, is an example of how a frontier can quickly jump nearly 2000 miles over an unoccupied country. There has been no other phenomenon like this in American history, and it is doubtful if world history offers a parallel case. It is significant that the immigrants went all this distance to a wooded and well-watered environment similar in practically all respects to that which they had known in the East. In fact, they passed over the fertile prairie and plains of the Midwest, where agricultural opportunities were as good as they were on the Pacific Coast, where everyone was headed. It has been customary to consider the trip over the Oregon Trail as a heroic act, and it was. But in another sense, it registered a lack of sufficient heroism to lead the people to undertake to live in the vast country that they traversed. In reality, they were seeking a familiar environment and avoiding the necessity of working out new ways on the plains. Their heroism lay in getting to Oregon and not in living there. The deserts, waterless drives, sandstorms, treacherous quicksands in rivers, prairie fires, hostile Indians and stampeding buffalo on the plains were all part of that great obstacle. The pioneers were bound for the land where the simple plow, the scythe, the ox and the horse could be used according to the tradition that had been worked out in two centuries of pioneering in a wooded country.

In a way, the plains made such a long leap possible. If in one sense they were an obstacle, in another they were a highway for travel. Had the region instead been heavily forested and well watered, there never would have been an Oregon Trail, for there would have been no reason for one. People would have found the land equally desirable all along the route, and the frontier would have advanced westward in the orderly manner in which it had come from the Atlantic to the edge of the timber in Missouri. The whole round of life would have been different from what it became. Had the Great Plains been heavily timbered, the wagon road to Oregon would have been almost physically impossible. The labor of opening up a road of that length through forests would have required a tremendous financial outlay, daunting even the most visionary pioneers.

However, since the rivers were not navigable, the mode of travel on the Great Plains became different from what people were accustomed to in the East. Travel over long distances east of the plains was usually by boat, whereas on the plains it had to be done wholly by land. The difficulty of land transportation, combined with the scarcity of water, accounts for most of the hardships of travel on the plains. In the East, there were ship captains and rivermen who were half horse and half alligator, and gamblers, river pirates, exploding boilers, treacherous shoals, snags and floods; in the West there were prairie schooners, bullwhackers, buffalo hunters, Indian scouts, sandstorms and stampedes.

Though it would not be exploited as such for many years, the Columbia River was a tremendous waterway. It has been said that from the Cascades westward over the Oregon Trail, 'you are not following a river, you are skirting the shores of a lake called a river. In any other land, these rocky points jutting out in the Columbia would be called capes. These islets in Europe would be independent principalities. It was because of the vast width of the river that canoes, rafts, cedar boats, [and] fir dugouts clung close to the shoreline. It was unsafe to thwart across these wide waters in wind or whip of tides.'

Above: A cow with seven small boys on her back posed in front of a schoolhouse in Okanogan, Washington for Frank Matsura in 1907.

Facing page: In 1907, the steamer *Expansion* made weekly trips on the Yellowstone River between Mondak and Glendive in Montana. The riverboat also carried freight for the lower Yellowstone reclamation project. Similar steamers worked the Columbia out of Portland.

Above: **Men gathered around the fire-place at Sawtell's Ranch at Henry's Lake, Fremont County, Idaho Territory in 1872.**

Lewis and Clark hugged the north shore going west and the south shore coming back east. The Astorians 10 years later did the same. The pioneers did both except that 'the cow column'—a name for all stock, oxen, horses and mules—kept to the narrow game trail below the modern Interstate Highway 84 on the south shore, because Indian villages dotted the north shore in an almost continuous line.

Nevertheless, few lives were lost from Indian raids or rough waters west of the Cascades. The rivers pouring into the Columbia—the Hood and Willamette from the south, the Yakima and the Cowlitz from the north, led to some of the most fertile areas in the world. They were described as 'hidden vales of a paradise.' Up these rivers, the pioneers found fertile plains, which became their first settlements. In the midst of such fertile plains sprang up such modern cities as Eugene, Salem, Yakima and Portland.

In 1843, a certain Mrs Dye recalled her impressions of an eruption of Oregon's formidable Mt Hood volcano:

'Old Waskema, returning with berries from Mt Hood, had seen the immigrants in bateaux going down to Fort Vancouver. Waskema set out for Fort Vancouver.

'It was a dark and heavy day. Not even when the great forest fire came down and threatened the fort had it been so oppressive. Dr McLaughlin went out to observe the lurid sky. Candles were lit in the hall, and the cattle came lowing up from the marshes at midday. The air was full of fine, light ashes that fell over a radius of 50 miles. For the first time in the memory of man, the white robes of Mt Hood were blackened with dust.

'Down by the boathouse, Dr McLaughlin saw old Waskema landing from her canoe. With the kindness of heart that would not slight even a withered old squaw, he advanced and took her hand. "Well, what's the good word, grandmother?"

'The decrepit old figure tried to straighten itself. In spite of her taciturnity, the white-headed Eagle had won the heart of old Waskema. A smile that was a pathetic contraction of leathern muscles long unused to laughter danced over her face and was gone. In a sepulchral tone, shaking her bony finger, pointing to the erupting mountain, the old squaw spoke words which were prophetic of the evil days that befell from 1847 to 1856 in raid and massacre. The attitude, the tone, the darkness, all corresponded with the gloom of the doctor's spirit. Only too well he knew that with this influx of Americans, the Hudson Bay's regime was over. A wind loaded with frost blew down from Mt Hood.'

The pioneers found Oregon and Washington to be a veritable cornucopia. There were raspberry, loganberry, blackberry and strawberry areas, with berries of a delicious flavor unknown elsewhere. The same was true of the fisheries. At Astoria, or up on the San Juans, they found clams more delicate than any other seafood. In other localities not a hundred miles away, a clam is just a clam—good, poor or indifferent. The same is true of silver salmon and deep-sea trout. In the 172 San Juan Islands, there were many harbors between crab-shaped coastlines where pioneers found a harbor famed for its trout, another for its silver salmon.

The Oregon of the pioneers' 'Promised Land' would be about the size of France with parts of Switzerland and Italy included. It was hard for Easterners to understand such dimensions, especially to grasp them in terms of farms, mines, timberland and fisheries. Some of the best wheat lands and fruit territory were in what is called the dry zone. The greatest wealth of mines and timberland was in the mountain wilderness, where pinnacled rocks seemed to bar human efforts.

Though Fort Vancouver (now Vancouver, Washington) seemed to mark the end of the Oregon Trail and of the long trek westward, the pioneers had to pick their

homesteads like an oasis in a wilderness. From Fort Vancouver to the ocean, the Columbia River takes a great bend north almost as confusing as the canyons of Snake River. To the east of the great bend are Mount Adams, Mount St Helen's and Mount Rainier, that hang like opal domes dyed in rose on the northeastern sky. 'You will mistake them at first for clouds set on fire by the sun,' wrote one early traveler. Each mountain pours its floods of thawed snow into the Columbia, which runs through the long ramparts of rocky foothills that divert its torrents through canyons and narrow passes to the Cowlitz River at Longview. The Chchalis cuts across to the Pacific Ocean by Gray's Harbor, site of Aberdeen and Hoquiam, two tidewater cities. The Snokomish and the Skykomish and the Snoqualami rivers pass from the main Cascades.

Portland really marks the western end of the Oregon Trail, but it does not mark the end of the Overland Trail. Lewis and Clark and the Astorians went on down the Columbia to the Pacific. Today, US Highway 30 follows their river trail. So do the railroads lining the broad waters of the river no longer descending the rock steps of stairways from the Cascade Mountains, but resembling more the majestic entrance of channels from tidewater than an inland river.

From the Pioneer Monument crowning the hill at Astoria is a vista of 200 miles of the Pacific Ocean, or 100 miles *from* the Pacific. As the War Memorial Monument at Kansas City stands on the site of the beginning of the Overland Trail, so does the Pioneer Monument mark the terminus of the great adventure. Between the two beautiful obelisks lies a century of heroism.

Above: **In this scene photographed on 20 September 1888 by NB Miller, crews at the Northern Pacific docks in Tacoma, Washington Territory are shipping the first cargo of halibut caught in Puget Sound by the crew of the schooner *Oscar & Hattie*.**

CALIFORNIA AND THE GOLD RUSH

Above: 'California or Bust' was the cry of treasure seekers who headed West.

Facing page: This photograph of Dutch Flat in California's Placer County was taken in 1855, six years after the gold rush.

It can be said that the period from 1769 to 1821–the half century from the founding of the missions to the end of Spanish rule–was the 'Golden Age' of California. A chain of Franciscan missions extended up the coast along El Camino Real (Royal Road), each link a day's journey apart. This Royal Road was indeed a peaceful route as it wound between the mountains and the ocean. Each mission, with its white walls and red-tiled roof, was built around a central plaza, hedged with roses and set within silvery olive orchards and orange trees.

Life was pleasant for the Spaniards on the great ranches granted to army officers and other favorites of the king or the viceroy of New Spain. Families were large, but cattle and sheep roamed the hills and food was plentiful. Many household tasks were carried out on the verandas around the central courtyards of the houses. The annual supply ship from New Spain brought tools and implements, brass and silver ornaments for church and home, and silks, velvets and brocades for church vestments and fine garments. They made their own linen and woolen cloth, harnesses and saddles, soft moccasins, and the chairs and bedsteads of wood and rawhide. They ground their own corn meal and flour. Dancing and open-handed hospitality prevailed at the annual rodeos, when livestock was rounded up and branded.

For the Indians, however, life was not so agreeable. Most never became wholly resigned to mission life, or to virtual slavery on the ranchos. Measles, pneumonia and other European diseases killed large numbers, causing a great deal of superstitious terror toward newcomers. Frequent revolts were brutally suppressed by the soldiers stationed at the presidios.

When the Mexicans won independence from Spain and took control of California in 1821, they halted the work of the Franciscans, and in 1833 they began to secularize the cities and towns that had grown up around the missions. Seizing church lands, they allowed the fields to run to weeds and permitted 30,000 Indian converts to leave the missions.

The grip of Mexico soon weakened, however, as foreign influence grew. British ships anchored in California harbors. France and Russia also looked upon the province with interest. As early as 1796, Ebenezer Dorr, a Boston skipper, had sailed into

Above: This old cut shows the place at Sutter's Mill in California where James Marshall made his 1848 discovery.

Monterey Bay and traded with the settlers. Other Yankee captains followed, despite Spanish laws against foreign trade. They bargained for sea otter furs, wheat, wool, hides and tallow in exchange for American goods. One such visit is vividly described in Richard Henry Dana's book *Two Years Before the Mast*.

American fur trappers began to enter from the East. Jedediah Smith braved blizzards and starvation in the High Sierra to scout the Cajon Pass into southern California in 1826 and explored the Sacramento Valley northward into Oregon. Joseph Walker, another trapper, discovered Yosemite Valley and the Walker Pass into San Jacinto Valley. Some of the traders and trappers married daughters of California ranch owners and became very influential. Others, returning east, spread word of the rich land whose Mexican rulers were too incompetent to defend it.

Imperial Russia also recognized the weakness of the Californians. Arriving in San Francisco in 1806 to buy supplies for the fur-trading post at Sitka, Alaska, Nicolai Petrovich Rezanov paved the way for the establishment, six years later, of Rossiya (Fort Ross), an outpost near the Russian River, north of San Francisco. He became engaged to Concepcion Arguello, daughter of San Francisco's Spanish *comandante*, but died while crossing Siberia to obtain the czar's consent to his marriage to a woman of another faith. When Concepcion learned of his death, she entered a convent. Gertrude Atherton told her story in her novel *Rezanov*. Supplies for Sitka were grown in California after 1812, and a wealth of California sea lion and sea otter furs was shipped to China at a great profit.

In 1841, convinced that California would soon belong to the United States, Russia sold Fort Ross to John Augustus Sutter. Captain Sutter (1803-1880), a resourceful pioneer of Swiss parentage, ruled like a feudal lord over the 97,000 acres of land he owned in the Sacramento Valley called New Helvetia (New Switzerland). His name would soon become legend in the history of California and the story of the opening of the American West.

Americans, too, were starting to come overland to California. A southern fork left the Oregon Trail at Fort Hall, north of the Great Salt Lake, and became the California Trail. It was less traveled in the 1840s because at that time Oregon, not California, was United States territory, and because the Sierra Nevada were a grueling, and often deadly, obstacle. One of the most tragic of such fates befell the Donner party, whose 45 survivors out of the original 87 were rescued from the blizzards of a Sierra Nevada winter by Sutter's guides in 1847.

The trickle of immigrants into California would soon become a flood. The reason would not be its orange groves, the rich fields of the Central Valley or even the seafood-rich coastal waters. It would be gold.

James A Dana had discovered gold in northern California in 1841. The next year Francisco Lopez, a sheepherder, caused a little excitement when he found gold near Los Angeles. But it was not until 24 January 1848 when James Marshall, a carpenter at John Sutter's sawmill near Coloma, found gold in the millrace in the American River, that the famous California gold rush was launched.

James W Marshall was born in Hope township, Hunterdon county, New Jersey on 10 May 1812. Little is known of his early childhood, but he was apprenticed to learn the wagon and coach-making trade when very young, and became a careful and expert workman. When he finished with his apprenticeship, he caught the 'Western fever' and went to Indiana to 'grow up with the country.' Soon afterward, he went to Illinois, and in 1840 he made a other move, this time beyond the Missouri River, where he bought a farm near what is now Leavenworth, Kansas. He remained here until 1843, and was obtaining financial success.

In May, 1844, his was one of about 100 wagons that set out for the Pacific Ocean. The original intention of these emigrants was to reach California, but Marshall and about 40 others decided to branch off and proceed to Oregon, and then go on to California, if their interests should so incline them. Even though Indians were known to be troublesome at that time, the wagon train never suffered an attack during the entire trip West.

Dissatisfied with his prospects in Oregon after spending the winter there, Marshall decided to make his way to California. He arrived at Cache Creek, about 40 miles from Sutter's New Helvetia in June 1845. Soon afterward, Marshall met Captain Sutter, and about the same time bought land on Butte Creek in what is now Butte County.

In the summer of 1846, the Mexican population began to anticipate a time when the American residents would outnumber them if emigration were not stopped, and began to organize to stem the tide of Americans entering California. Force was threatened. John C Fremont was then at Sutter Buttes with an insignificant number of troops under his command, and Sutter, Marshall, and all the other Americans within reach, joined Fremont in defense of their countrymen. Marshall served as a soldier until the surrender of General Andres Pico in March 1847, closed the war. He returned to Fort Sutter to find his ranch devastated and his stock stolen. With no better prospects in sight, Marshall accepted the position of overseeing the Indians employed by Captain Sutter at Sutter's mill.

On the morning of 19 January 1848, after the water had been turned off by shutting down the mill's headgate, Marshall and Peter Wimmer were walking leisurely along the tailrace of the mill, where the water had run all night, and washed away all the loose dirt which had been dug up by the men the night before. Marshall spotted a shiny object lying on a flat rock close to the side of the tailrace. Picking it up and turning it over in his hands, it required no great stretch of imagination to consider it a very remarkable representation of the 'Bear' that had adorned the flag he had lately helped to raise as an emblem of California independence.

The rock attracted his attention more because of its peculiar shape and queer likeness to a bear than for its probable value. Handing it to Wimmer, he said, 'What do you think of that?'

Wimmer took it in his hand and felt its weight and said, 'That must be gold. I would take my pay in that metal.' He became convinced that what his wife had so often said must be true: the specks of bright metal that they often spotted in the river must have been gold.

Jennie Wimmer was preparing to make a kettle of soap that day, and the two men had put her kettle of lye on the fire before they left the cabin. Marshall said, 'Well Peter, we will send that to Jennie, and let her boil it in her soap kettle all day, and see if it will tarnish it.'

When Jennie poured the soap into a trough, she found the beautiful nugget, polished bright by the action of the lye. Seizing it, she threw it on the table before her husband and Marshall, shouting aloud, as she had from the first, 'There is your nugget, and it is pure gold.'

Peter Wimmer agreed with his wife that indeed the nugget was gold. Marshall was reticent in expression, but seemed impressed with the possibility that that it might,

Above: **Panning for gold on one of the tributaries of the American River in the Sierra Nevada.**

indeed, be gold. Over the next five days, other small nuggets were collected and Marshall took them with him to Fort Sutter. Tests at the fort proved that the rock was truly gold, and Captain Sutter accompanied him to Coloma on his return. Upon their arrival at the cabin, Marshall handed Jennie Wimmer the nugget she had tested in her kettle of soap, and said, 'Here, Jennie. This will make you a nice ring, and it shall be yours.' Jennie kept it and always took great pride in showing off the first nugget of gold found in California.

James W Marshall died alone in his cabin at Kelsey's Diggings in El Dorado County in 1885, with not even enough wealth to defray the expenses of his simple burial. He had never been prosperous. In 1877, the California legislature voted him a pension of $1200 per year to continue for four years. In 1887, $5,000 was appropriated for a monument, which was unveiled on 3 May 1890 atop Marshall Hill, overlooking the point where the first nugget had been discovered.

It has been written that humankind's grandest achievements and highest development are found in close proximity to a gold mine. Historians recalled that rarely has a nation been prominent in art and science which has not had stores of the yellow metal to draw upon, and in those instances when people had invaded the strongholds of other nations, and carried off the gold accumulated by *them* over time.

The discovery of gold in California came exactly at the right time, and the flow was so abundant that for a time gold was the cheapest known commodity in California. In some places lumber was sold for 50 cents a pound, flour at three dollars per pound, and other things in proportion. These times were financially unhealthy, as is always the case when the necessities of life cost anything approaching their weight in gold.

So doubtful was Marshall initially of the value of his discovery that he made no effort to prove that it was gold until several days later. It was not until the first week in February that Sutter and Marshall were back at the mill, that they made public their discovery of gold. Soon after, the news found its way to San Francisco and gold fell as low as four dollars per ounce in exchange for supplies. Early in May, the editor of the *California Star* went to the mines, presumably to gather facts of interest to his readers. He announced in his paper on 6 May that he had returned, and on 20 May noticed the departure of a fleet of launches, 'laden with superlatively silly people' on their way to the mines.

When the news reached the East, it spread like a prairie wildfire. Companies were organized in every city of the north and south, and in many cases incorporated, for the development of mines in the Far West. By the spring of 1849, more than 30,000 ambitious men had gathered at Independence, Missouri, Leavenworth, Kansas, St Joseph, Missouri and Council Bluffs, Iowa, ready to attack the mysteries of the plains as soon as vegetation began to send forth the green shoots of spring. The great majority of these men were not going to stay. They weren't traveling to California to become Californians but to become *rich*. The forty-niners were going for the gold and then they planned to return home. Nevertheless, many *did* stay to become Californians and many of these became *rich* Californians. It was now inevitable–if it hadn't *already* been inevitable–that California was going to become an American state very soon.

Sutter's part in Americanizing California was not as important as that of John C Fremont. Fremont had already won national fame by being the first to make a scientific survey of the Pacific and by writing vividly of his explorations. Fremont refused the Mexican order to leave California, and helped to instigate the 1846 American short-lived revolt in Sonoma known as the 'Bear Flag Revolt.'

Left: California Governor George Pardee (center) and his friends are given a lift to his favorite fishing hole by the Southern Pacific Railroad.

Facing page: A statue of James Marshall commemorating his discovery of gold in 1848 that sparked the 1849 California gold rush.

In that same year, the United States had declared war against Mexico, and after several fierce confrontations, the invading army, under General Stephen Watts Kearny of California, took California. By the treaty of Guadalupe-Hidalgo (1848), California became a United States territory. Two years later, on 9 September 1850, it was admitted to the Union as the thirty-first state as part of the Missouri Compromise of 1850.

William H Seward referred to the new state as 'the youthful queen of the Pacific, in robes of freedom gorgeously inlaid with gold.' When in 1848 Fremont refused to recognize the authority of General Kearny, who had assumed the office of governor, he was court-martialed and left the Army. Fremont continued his colorful, but turbulent, career as a senator from California between 1850 and 1851, as the Republican party presidential candidate in 1856, as a major general during the Civil War, as a railroad builder and victim of the financial panic of 1873 and finally as governor of Arizona between 1878 and 1872.

All parts of the nation shared in the excitement of the gold rush of 1848-1849. Crews deserted their ships, farmers threw aside their plows and merchants boarded up their stores to rush out to California. They came around Cape Horn, across the plains and across the isthmus of Panama. The swiftest California clippers made the Cape Horn trip in three months, carrying fortune seekers able to pay dearly for first-class passage, but ordinary ships took six to nine months for the voyage. Hardy pioneers traveled overland, taking with them their cattle and farm implements. Prairie schooners assembled by the score along the Mississippi and in Kansas, organized in great caravans for protection, and lumbered toward the setting sun.

About 50,000 immigrants started out in the spring of 1849, eager to cross the Sierra Nevada before snow blocked the passes. Salt Lake City, just settled by the Mormons, was a halfway station on the long and dangerous journey. Countless forty-niners, well equipped and expertly guided, made the five month trip without mishap. But many thousands more were killed by Indians or died from cholera, scurvy, thirst and hunger while crossing the parched deserts and climbing the long, winding trails over the mountains. Because the Panama route was shortest and seemed easiest, it was most crowded, but hundreds died of yellow fever while transiting the isthmus.

The early miners of California depended entirely upon placer mining, or gold found in the sand and gravel along streams and gulches, or where the surface had been washed down from the mountains and deposited on the flats. For the first few years after the initial discovery, there was no quartz mining, and no mine shafts penetrated the hills. It was simply so easy to pan for gold that digging for it didn't seem worth the trouble. Even in 1850, it was estimated that only $40,000 was invested in quartz mining machinery in the whole state.

The first nugget of sufficient size to create more than a mere local sensation was spotted by a soldier in the Mokelumne River while he was taking a drink. The nugget weighed nearly 25 pounds. The nugget was sent to New York, where it was placed on exhibit, creating such a furor that it was probably the cause of many a man striking out for California.

The largest mass of gold ever found in California was dug out at Carson Hill in Calaveras County in 1854. It weighed 195 pounds. On 18 August 1860, WA Farish and Harry Warner took a mass of gold and quartz weighing 133 pounds from the Monumental quartz mine in Sierra County. Nuggets weighing 30 to 50 pounds were not uncommon.

Above: John Sontag of the firm of Evans & Sontag was shot to death in California for cheating on 14 September 1904. He was not yet dead when this picture was taken.

Left: Nevada City, California, circa 1893, was a thriving placer town that went mad for gold quartz mining. Some miners took to digging up the streets in search of gold when their old claims were exhausted.

Above: San Francisco at the turn of the century was a vital, ebullient city. This view from Nob Hill looks down California Street toward the bay, over the piers to Yerba Buena Island.

A cable car is visible in the lower right corner. Cable cars still serve the California Street line.

Facing page: Dick's Saloon & Restaurant, located at 43d and Point Lobos, was one of San Francisco's original 24-hour restaurants. It featured lagers of the Willows and Weiland breweries.

Of all the early western cities, San Francisco was the one that had to fight least for its place in the sun. Lady Luck smiled upon her, and she became the beneficiary of the rich commerce that flowed through the Golden Gate into one of the greatest natural harbors in the world. This vast harbor with its mile-wide gate had curiously eluded the first five explorers who sailed along the coast of California, including Sir Francis Drake, who anchored at Drake's Bay a few miles to the north, a body of water which had previously been charted by the Spanish explorer Sebastian Rodrigues Cermeno, who named it Puerto de San Francisco.

It was not until 1776 that the Spanish decided that the shore of the large body of water was in reality the proper place to establish the Laguna de Nuestra Señora de los Dolores (Mission Dolores), the northernmost of their string of missions, all a day's journey apart, extending along the El Camino Real (the Royal Highway), north from San Diego. The city of San Francisco grew up away from the mission on the shores of the bay, when immigrants began to erect trading houses on land which was covered with a fragrant mint called Yerba Buena ('the good mint').

San Francisco was little more than a sleepy village when Marshall found the famous first nugget of gold. When his discovery was made known, it threw millions of men the world over into a fever of excitement and started the greatest movement of people centered on a single goal since the crusades of the Middle Ages. It destroyed the California that then existed, despoiling the empires of Sutter and Vallejo by turning their lands over to hordes of Yankee squatters. It caused the currency markets of the world to tremble, raised the United States to new heights as a monetary power and attracted adventurous men to California who would eventually develop her resources and center the financial power and transportation systems of the entire West in the fledgling city of San Francisco.

By November 1848, there were 600 ships in San Francisco harbor, each of which had brought its full quota of passengers. Forty-two thousand came overland in 1849, 9000 from Mexico. They found San Francisco to be a strange city, sandy, windswept, straggling and unkempt, rising from low shore lands to nearby high hills. The harbor was crowded with deserted ships, several of which had been drawn up to the shore to serve as warehouses, and one as a hotel. On the high hills, wherever there was room for foothold, the newcomers perched their houses, usually strips of canvas tacked around redwood posts, which when lighted up at night, made the town look as if it were hung with gigantic Chinese lanterns. The streets in the level part of the city alongside the bay were literally seas of mud in which unwary pedestrians sometimes actually drowned at night. One corner bore a sign, 'This Street Is Impassable–Not Even Jackassable.'

The forty-niners built a city on the sand hills of San Francisco. The harbor then came up as far as Montgomery Street, and the huts of the squatters extended from the end of the business section around Portsmouth Square into the district now bounded by First, Second, Market and Mission Streets, known as Happy Valley. Telegraph Hill swarmed with ex-convicts, thieves, cutthroats, and ticket-of-leave men from Australia and bore the name of Sidney Town, while at its foot was a crowded settlement of Chileans–as all South Americans were called by the forty-niners. Huts and shacks were made of canvas or any other material that could be patched together, though the rich who lived around Portsmouth Square had their houses built in Boston and imported in sections. The foundations of small buildings were apt to be of such strange material as tons of wire sieves or barrels of beef. The salvation of this flimsy town was the keen,

Above: **Crossing the Sierra Nevada was no simple feat for the miners, settlers and railroad builders.**

tonic salt wind that blew over it and kept it fresh. An epidemic would have wiped out the population, for to be sick in the California of those days, with few doctors or medicines and unspeakably inadequate hospitals, was to die. Although it was spared epidemics, San Francisco was made to suffer trial by fire. Six times flames swept over the old town and six times it was rebuilt. The city chose the phoenix for its crest.

The streets bustled with a motley crowd of jostling men, most of whom were young–to be 30 was considered aged–who rejoiced in wearing the picturesque slouch hats or sombreros, wool shirts and top boots of the mines and in letting their beards grow. There was a liberal sprinkling of other costumes as well. The Chinese wore basket hats and hundreds of Mexican gamblers wore high black beavers, white shirts and diamond studs. France sent the new land 'several thousand lying men and corrupt women,' embarking them at the expense of the government. Italy sent musicians and also farmers, who soon became rich, selling eggs at from $6 to $12 a dozen. Germany sent dairymen, barbers and laundrymen, the last of whom inherited a profitable trade, for San Francisco once sent its laundry to Hawaii and China because the local price was $10 a dozen.

Never did men become affluent so quickly as in the California of 1849. Although some never made more than a day laborer's wages, thousands struck it rich. Nuggets worth thousands of dollars were found, and the miners, washing the gravel in creek beds using shallow circular pans and large wooden rockers, discovered pay dirt yielding fortunes.

In the first five years of the gold rush, nearly 1.25 billion dollars worth of gold was taken out of the soil of California, and much of it was spent in Sacramento and the mining camps which rejoiced in such euphonious titles as Fleatown, Hangtown, Whiskey Gulch, You Bet, Poison Switch, You Be Dam, Delirium Tremens, Shirttail Canyon and Lousy Level. But it was to San Francisco, known universally as 'the City,' and still referred to by that title in the West, that the miners traveled for their more exuberant and extravagant periods of relaxation and the city became known throughout the world for wildness, boisterousness and extravagance. Gold dust was the medium of exchange, a pinch taken from the miner's pouch being the price of a drink, and bartenders won, or failed to win, their jobs as a result of their demonstration in reply to the question, 'How much can you raise in a pinch?'

Prices were always high, but they fluctuated violently as the market was alternately skimped and glutted through the arrival of ships with various kinds of cargo. Flour would sell for $27 a barrel one week and less than half that price the next. Cargoes were often thrown into the bay because the cost of paying the excessively high wages required to land was more than they were worth. Rooms in the good hotels cost $250 a month. A large canvas tent used by gamblers rented for $40,000 a year. The best restaurants charged $5 a meal and General Vallejo recounts that a man could sell a wagonload of fish caught in the bay for $5000 up in the mines.

Inevitably, San Francisco became glutted with adventurers and criminals from all over the world. So flagrant did the outrages of these men become and so impotent was the local government to cope with them that citizens took the law into their own hands and organized the Vigilantes. Among the scoundrels who came to San Francisco there were an equal number of talented, legitimate entrepreneurs. Every day saw the arrival of others, who were to remain long after the gold rush was over to make California great. From New York State came the young lawyers Leland Stanford and Mark Hopkins, and also that native of Connecticut, Collis P Huntington. Charles Crocker,

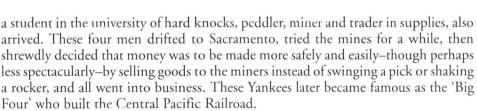

a student in the university of hard knocks, peddler, miner and trader in supplies, also arrived. These four men drifted to Sacramento, tried the mines for a while, then shrewdly decided that money was to be made more safely and easily—though perhaps less spectacularly—by selling goods to the miners instead of swinging a pick or shaking a rocker, and all went into business. These Yankees later became famous as the 'Big Four' who built the Central Pacific Railroad.

James C 'Big Jim' Flood, an Irish-born New Yorker of 23, landed on the muddy streets of San Francisco in 1849 and met William S O'Brien, another young Irishman, who proposed that they earn their fortunes with the towel and bottle instead of the pick and shovel by operating a saloon in San Francisco. There was also the keen-eyed Adolph Sutro, who came from Aix-la-Chapelle by way of New York and Panama, and who spent his evenings studying how to reclaim the treasures of gold that were lost in the crude rockers of the early miners. Around Flood & O'Brien's bar and in their lunchroom, where a particularly succulent fish stew was served, there gathered other men whose names were later to become famous: Darius Ogden Mills, financier; Elias Jackson ('Lucky') Baldwin, miner and landowner; John P Jones, future senator from Nevada; and William C Ralston, destined to become head of the largest banking monopoly in the West. All these men were adventurers who sought gold, and when they later came to dominate the affairs of California, they gave the state that reputation for breezy recklessness, daring schemes and bold operations which it has never lost.

Above left: Lefty Lamon's log cabin was the first built in Yosemite Valley, California in 1895. Their work completed, two men sit on stumps in front of the finished product.

Above: Railroad baron Mark Hopkins' grand residence atop Nob Hill in San Francisco, like Lamon's log cabin (*above, left*), was built in 1889.

Like Lamon's home, Hopkins' house was made of wood, and as such, it was destroyed in the fire that followed the 1906 earthquake. Today this is the site of the Mark Hopkins Hotel.

CROSSING THE PLAINS

Above: Travelling overland involved many forms of transportation, from covered wagons to–believe it or not–wheelbarrows!

Facing page: An immigrant family poses with their covered wagon on the Nebraska plains.

The gold rush of 1848-1849 touched off a westward migration the likes of which could have never been imagined a few years before. Estimates of those on the Overland Trail in 1849 range as high as 50,000, and roughly 20,000 annually in the years following. They included forty-niners–wild-eyed opportunists, hardworking would-be miners and crafty entrepreneurs–and they included the families under the tents of their covered wagons, with cows for milk trailing behind. When one adds these totals to the Mormon migration to Utah and the Oregon pioneers, the Overland Trail and the opening of the American West were all part of the great epic of a nation.

In 1847, 2000 Mormons were on the Trail, some using only hand carts to cross the plains. By 1856, even greater numbers of Mormons were on the Trail. By 1847, 5000 Oregon pioneers were on the Trail and a thousand soon-to-be Californians, though gold had not yet become the magnet of the stampede that followed two years later. However, the size of this migration did not lessen the hardships for its participants. Storms broke the heat with terrible violence and lightning crackled.

The rains did dampen the dust and permit a good wash of faces and clothing, as well as swelling the dried wagon frames which had been threatening to rattle apart from sheer sunscorch. Repairs had to be made at intervals few and far between, as the pioneers knew they had to be sure and make it across South Pass before snow blocked the way.

Next to the buffalo stampedes, the overlanders dreaded the floods and the whirling tornadoes of wind preceding fierce rainstorms when tent pegs were torn from the dry sands and tents on wagons almost tipped to the blast of the winds. Like their animals, the campers had to learn not to lose their heads in the confusion, but to close up ranks, turn their backs to howling winds and hold fast to tent ropes until the storm had passed. Fort Kearney, the first Army post on the Overland Trail, was really established like Leavenworth, that is, to act as a boundary between marauding Indians north and south, especially to protect trails toward Montana and as an outer patrol for Indian Territory. Why it was not exterminated in the few years of its existence, is one of the heroic annals of the Army. Jim Bridger, the famous scout, was employed at the fort as a

Above: Freight wagon teams crossing the Rocky Mountains at Ute Pass.

Facing page: A noon meal in Ferdinand Hayden's US Geological Survey camp at Red Buttes in Wyoming Territory on 24 August 1870. Hayden himself is at the far end of the table in a dark jacket and the photographer, WH Jackson, stands at far right.

guide in the 1860s, and he advised all teamsters and mule wranglers for the Army to park wagons in a natural wall of protection from Indian fire. He kept telling the commander that Indian spies were behind every sage clump until the officers thought 'old Jim had Indians on the brain.' Still, as many as seven soldiers a day had been buried as Fort Kearney was being built, victims of Indian spies.

On 21 December 1866, Colonel Fetterman and 81 men had been sent out to protect a mule train carrying timber, but went out improperly equipped. The soldier horsemen on their skittish horses were clumsy riders compared to the Indians, who could ride bareback and duck as they fired with guns or arrows, and could ride their ponies in a zigzag pattern to avert the slower aim of the soldiers, who had been trained to dismount and take sure aim.

The Indians rushed the troopers and then feigned a retreat that drew Fetterman in pursuit to a hornets' nest. He and his company disappeared over a ridge. Soldiers back at the fort heard quick, desperate firing, followed by a sickening, awful, prolonged, dead silence. Lieutenant Eyck and 54 men hurried in the direction of the battle and found 81 mutilated bodies on the hillside. Not a soul had escaped to tell the tale of the last man's shot.

Of course, the Sioux captured the battalions' guns and bullets, and Chief Red Cloud, retreating in a whirl with his warriors, must have smiled at the white man's rashness for running into his well laid trap. Major Powell formed fortifications out of his wagon boxes by setting them on their sides and having a relay of extra rifles set up behind each sharpshooter. These were stacked upright, three and four for each man. It would be rapid-fire, the swiftest the Indians had ever experienced. Never dreaming he could not repeat his easy victory over 81 men, now in August 1867, against 30 men, Chief Red Cloud hurled his warriors down and led the whirling charge in person. The troops were now armed with Springfield repeaters. Red Cloud's warriors shot five flaming arrows inside the wagon box fort until the ground smoked and the grass caught fire. Not knowing other rifles stood stacked ready at hand, Red Cloud now charged his full force of 3000 at the encircled whites. The fire arrows came flaming in to hit the dust inside the square, but the sharpshooters behind the wagon boxes, now on sides with floors of iron, broke Red Cloud's arrow showers, and the bullets coming from the shelter of the lined boxes picked off the warriors zig-zagging as they charged. Powell lost only three men, the Sioux 1137. If that victory had been followed up instantly, it may have averted even more fearful massacres in a few years to the north, but Washington did not take any further action.

The 300 miles between Fort Kearney and Laramie, Wyoming, was the most dramatic on the Trail. Along this section, all prongs began to fork to their different destinations, southwest to Santa Fe, west to Salt Lake and California, north to Montana and northwest to Snake River and Oregon. The overlanders soon forgot the smell of the sweet clover meadows scented with the nectar of white, red and pink blooms where the big bumblebees make more of a merry din than honey, and the gorgeous butterflies have velvet cloaks woven of pansy petals in blue and yellow and gold. To this day, hummingbirds are found in abundance in the clover fields of the Kansas and Platte rivers.

Beyond Laramie were foothills scant of grass, but covered with cactus and sagebrush. Here was the Great American Desert of red buttes and fantastic sandstone chimneys, with dust as fine as flour and small pebbles whipped to a pepper of sand-hail

Above: **Frank E Webner was one of the many scrappy adventure seekers to sign on to be a Pony Express rider in 1861.**

in the wind. Soon the eye became aware that the clouds to the west were not all moving. Some stand majestically still, not clouds at all, but the shining mountains of the Rockies. Beyond the Rockies lay the dreadful Great Basin, the most deserted corner of the Great American Desert.

Past the basin lay the Sierra Nevada, the final obstacle, upon which the Donner party suffered so terribly a year before Marshall found gold. The stupendous range of the Sierra Nevada, attaining an altitude of 14,500 feet, presents hundreds of miles of a forbidding, precipitous face. Feasible passes were rare. At the time when Fremont made his attempt to cross, they were practically unknown to white men, as the mountain range had never been mapped. On the basin side, the passes opened low, while on the western side they were high up on the long and gradual slopes. In winter, the snows on top of the Sierra lie extremely deep, the cold becomes intense, and following trails hidden beneath the snow is precarious. It was not until 1868, when the Central Pacific Railroad was completed, that it first became possible to ignore winter in crossing the mountains. Even then, the line was protected through many miles by massive timber sheds, fitting in places against the slopes of the mountains.

For the two decades following the gold rush, however, California lived the irony of being a popular destination and an America state, but a place that was so surely separated from the rest of the nation, it might as well have been located on the moon. The cities of the East were linked by roads, rail lines and the instantaneous communication of the telegraph. Communication with San Francisco, which was every bit as important a metropolis as Baltimore or Boston, took three months or longer.

As this distant, separate place grew in importance—both economically and culturally—the need for rapid communication became vital. The solution to this problem was innovative in the true spirit of the pioneers who opened the American West. Inaugurated in 1860, the Pony Express averaged 250 miles a day and traversed the distance between Sacramento and the Mississippi River in only 10 days!

The Pony Express developed some of the finest types of booted and spurred riders known to history; and nearly all passed to oblivion or died on duty in their boots. Only one—William F 'Buffalo Bill' Cody—went down in history by the showman's route. Yet there are many tales of riders who lost a leg or arm by being frozen as they reeled off the dizzy miles in winter blizzards. But they got the mail through, and for that duty received five dollars a day and keep. The Pony Express was, in some sections, the same trail followed by the Astorians, fur traders, Oregon pioneers and California forty-niners.

Few episodes in the West are so crammed with thrills as that of the Pony Express. Just before the Civil War, Fort Kearney, west of Omaha, counted 800 wagons with 10,000 oxen passing each day. Letters might cost $5 from New York to the Pacific Coast and might take six months or a year in transit. It was said that the representatives in Washington of the Western Territories might not receive mail from constituents until their term had expired.

Stage lines and covered wagons were already on the Trail when the Pony Express began. Of course, the Eastern senators and congressmen ridiculed the possibility of a new fast Pony Express, but the cost to the government of $2 million a year for mail service did ultimately convince them that something should be done to connect Pacific and Atlantic so that mail could travel faster and cheaper. The capital outlay involved by the private undertaking of the Pony Express was enormous. Cool-headed, lightweight young fellows were picked for riders from the Missouri to the Pacific.

Left: Mormon emigrants photographed in their covered wagon caravan by CW Carter in 1879.

Hardy, lean, fast horses–crossbred from the best plains cayuses and domestic racing strains–were selected. Nearly 200 changing stations were built, and 400 helpers and 80 riders were placed at these stations. Each rider's division was limited to 75 miles. Saddle, bridle and saddle bags could not exceed 13 pounds and the mail was limited to 20 pounds a runner. Riders could not weigh more than 130 pounds. The only arms they were allowed to carry were two revolvers and a sheathed knife. The mail was tied in waterproof bags.

Each rider had to take an oath: 'I do hereby swear, before the great and living God, that during my engagement, and while I am an employee of Russell, Majors & Faddell, I will under no circumstances use profane language; that I will drink no intoxicating liquors; that I will not quarrel or fight with any other employee of the firm, and that in every respect, I will conduct myself honestly, be faithful to my duties and so direct all my acts as to win the confidence of my employers. So help me God.' Often all that the emigrants saw was a flashing horseman riding at mad speed through the dust, who waved his hat, vanished and perhaps at the next turn of the trail ran into a peppering shot of an Indian raid, which he dodged by sheer speed or ducking down on the far side of his horse. He rode into the night, out of the night, through winter blizzard and summer heat.

Facing page: WH Jackson's photograph of the US Geological Survey of the Territories, conducted by Ferdinand Hayden, under way with its pack train on the trail between the Yellowstone and East Fork rivers in Wyoming Territory.

Below: An overview of Cheyenne in Wyoming Territory in 1876.

Right: An 1878 photograph of the *Rosebud*, the historic Missouri River boat that ran from Bismark, North Dakota, to Coalbanks, Montana, the head of the 753-mile-long navigable section of the 2315-mile-long river.

Facing page: The Overland Stage road between Ogden, Utah and Helena, Montana crossed the Beaver Head River at Point of Rocks by means of a plank bridge. WH Jackson took this photograph in 1871.

Below: A homestead overlooking the Bear River, which runs through the Cache Valley on the border between Idaho and Utah. The Shoshone Indians had once camped on this site, until Colonel Patrick Conner attacked them and drove them off in 1862.

THE TRANSCONTINENTAL RAILROAD

Above: Representatives of the press accompanying an excursion party to a point 275 miles west of Omaha, Nebraska Territory. This photo was taken for the Union Pacific Railroad by John Carbutt on 24 October 1866.

Facing page: A fanciful, nineteenth-century view showing a train embarking from frontier 'civilization' to follow the wagon train across the plains.

On a September morning in 1859, nine months before Abraham Lincoln was nominated for the office of President of the United States, he climbed to the top of a high cliff at Council Bluffs, Iowa, and looked westward across the plains. At his back was American civilization–the busy cities, rich commerce, fertile farms and comfortable homes of the young republic. Before him was a sparsely peopled land, beginning with the bare flood plains of the Missouri, through which the broad, sluggish, muddy river twisted its way. Close at hand, in the fields of wild grass and sunflowers below him, a few lonely, scattered cabins sent their columns of smoke drifting upward. And away to the west stretched the open country, flat, unbroken and interminable as a becalmed sea.

As he looked over those wide-spreading plains that morning and watched the meandering river which found its source a thousand miles to the north and west, Abraham Lincoln symbolized America. For America, too, was looking to the West and dreaming of its future. Pioneers had begun to cross the Mississippi River two generations before, in 1803, after Congress purchased the vast territory of Louisiana from France. Four decades later, settlers journeyed to the southwest, and in 1845 America acquired the plains of Texas. The next year, a long dispute with Great Britain over the western fur trade ended and Oregon was added, reaching north along the Pacific to the forty-ninth latitude.

In 1848, by cession from Mexico, California was acquired, and in 1853, with the Gadsden Purchase of a strip of Mexican desert, America became solidly completed from Atlantic to Pacific.

When gold was discovered in California in 1849 and later in Colorado in 1858, there already were rich farm lands waiting for the plow in green Oregon valleys and the plains of Texas swarmed with fat cattle. The fever of adventure spread throughout New England, the Midwest and South, and men by the thousands set out on the long overland journey to find a land of riches. For years an unbroken stream of covered wagons had been struggling across the broad plains over which Lincoln now stood, to California, Colorado and Oregon. These early emigrants encountered arduous travel conditions, tortuous roads and antagonistic Indians. Wagons sometimes stuck

Above: Photographed by John Carbutt in October 1866, the directors of the Union Pacific Railroad are seen here about 250 miles west of Omaha in what was then Nebraska Territory. The train in the background awaits this party of eastern industrialists.

Facing page: Union Pacific crews at Weber Canyon grading the line ahead as tracklayers work in the foreground. Along this stretch of track, known as the narrows, was some of the most difficult grading of the whole line.

in the mire, and the blanched bones of men and animals strewn along the trail were startling, although constant, reminders of the rigors of overland travel.

Lincoln knew all these things and more. He knew of the heated disputes in Congress over the political alignment of the new territories. He knew that the new lands were ready for orderly colonization by larger numbers of people than the covered wagons could ever carry, and that the things now needed for the development of the cities, towns and resources in America's vast new empire were men and money. Most of all, he knew that the first step in opening up the West must be the building of a railroad. A transcontinental railroad. A railroad that would stretch all the way to the Pacific Ocean.

No one doubted that the riches of the West must be brought to the doors of the East. The only question was, which doors? The South wanted the rails to extend westward from Texas to California, directing the commerce of the new territories to the port of New Orleans at the mouth of the Mississippi. The St Louis interests favored a route running southward from their city to California.

Kansas wished the railroad to run straight west over the back of the Rockies at its center near Denver and on to San Francisco. Chicago favored a line that would unite the Missouri River at Council Bluffs and Omaha with the harbor of San Francisco. The most northern route of all was that projected to join Lake Superior with Puget Sound and the Columbia River, and to connect with the East by means of steamers across the Great Lakes to Detroit.

While he was at Council Bluffs, Lincoln met the 28-year-old railroad surveyor Grenville M Dodge. He knew his subject thoroughly. In addition to his own surveys, he had read the reports and opinions of Fremont and the pioneer surveyors, Stanbury's studies of Salt Lake and other government documents. He also knew the route from Council Bluffs so well that he had made a map for emigrants which, he said, 'gave an itinerary showing each camping place all the way to California, giving the fords and where water and wood could be found. This map was published by the citizens of Council Bluffs for the purpose of controlling emigration. Since it was one of the first maps giving such information, it had a great influence in concentrating a large portion of the Oregon and California emigration at Council Bluffs after 1854.'

So sure was Dodge that this route was the predestined and logical way to the West that he filed a government claim on the Elkhorn River, 30 miles west of Omaha, and began his fight for the proposed Pacific railroad to pass through his property and up the valley of the Platte River. Soon afterward, the covered wagons, usually 20 in a train, having outfitted at Council Bluffs, began to roll past the Dodge cabin and to use his land for camping, since it was just far enough west of Omaha to provide a first night stopover. Dodge put all the information he had gained from his own investigation and from the experiences of others at Lincoln's disposal.

From Dodge, Lincoln learned that the route he proposed was the most practical and economical, and that buffalo, Indians and Mormon emigrants had already proved the trail up the Platte River valley to the Rockies to be the natural route to the West. The young surveyor believed that 'there was never any very great question, from an engineering point of view, as to where the line, crossing Iowa and going west from the Missouri River, should be placed. The Lord had so constructed the country that any engineer who failed to take advantage of the great open road out the Platte valley and then on to Salt Lake, would not have been fit to belong to the profession.'

Above: Samuel Reed, General Superintendent and Engineer of Construction for the Union Pacific.

Right: Theodore Judah surveyed the Central Pacific's route across the Sierra Nevada.

Facing page: The Union Pacific Railroad's paymaster's car at Blue Creek station. From 250 in 1865, the construction forces grew to 10,000 by completion of the transcontinental railroad in 1869. About one in four were track layers. The others were graders, teamsters, herdsmen, cooks, bakers, blacksmiths, bridge builders, carpenters, masons and clerks. On the average, they made three dollars a day. Many were Irish and most were veterans of the Civil War. When payday arrived, the money was passed out by the two clerks standing in the doorway.

In 1854, when the Kansas-Nebraska Act was passed, the southern route was permanently blocked, and with it Jefferson Davis' plan for the ultimate absorption of Mexico into the United States. It is also probable that the Act kept California in the Union, for had that state been joined to the South by commercial ties, it might well have seceded along with the Confederacy. Like the Midwest, whose sympathies had passed from the South to the North when northern railroads began to carry their trade away from New Orleans to New York, the new state of California now found its interests definitely allied with the North against any movement for secession.

The Union Pacific Railroad was chartered on 1 July 1862, and Congress left the choice of the eastern terminus to the President of the United States. Lincoln issued an executive order designating Council Bluffs, Iowa, and Grenville Dodge was soon helping to build the first railroad to the West. From Omaha, Nebraska, across the Missouri River from Council Bluffs, the road began to send its shining bands of steel westward to meet a second road, the Central Pacific, building east from Sacramento.

With the laying of the first rails, the way was finally opened for the building of the West. The days of covered wagon, Pony Express and straggling bands of weary, beleaguered emigrants would soon be over. It would be a hard seven years, but from the 1870s on, great hordes of colonists would make the western trip quickly and easily in a few days, and the crops and goods they produced in the new country would be speedily transported back to the centers of population in the East. As the rails pushed westward, the buffalo and the Indian would vanish. As the country became more and more cultivated, cattle would be driven from the free open range, mountains would be rifled of their coal and ore, waters of their fish and forests of their trees. The way would soon be ready for the second string of pioneers–the builders, businessmen, industrialists and promoters who would exploit the resources, build the cities and create America's new empire in the West.

Before this could happen, however, the railroad had to be built. The Union Pacific was only half of the project, and by the end of the 1860s, the race across the continent between the Union Pacific and the Central Pacific would become a spectacle, the likes of which the world had never seen.

In 1854, another man who was to have profound influence on the development of the West came to San Francisco. Theodore D Judah, like Grenville Dodge, was a civil engineer who conceived the idea of building the Pacific railroad. After failing to interest San Francisco financiers in the project, he was able to secure the backing of four prominent Sacramento merchants: Mark Hopkins, Collis P Huntington, Charles Crocker and Leland Stanford, whom he would turn into the greatest railroad builders in the country. When General William Tecumseh Sherman decided to build a California railroad from Sacramento east and north along the foothills to tap the rich placer mining country, with extensions running north, south and east, he made Judah his engineer. The problems of building a valley railroad were not sufficiently difficult to hold his interest, and he began to speculate on the possibility of building a railroad from the Pacific to the Atlantic, from San Francisco over the High Sierra. He crossed and recrossed the Sierra 23 times in order to locate the line across Dutch Flat. He then induced the state legislature to call a railroad convention, including delegates from Oregon, Arizona and Nevada, which met in San Francisco in 1859. In 1861, he was one of the incorporators of the Central Pacific Railroad.

Judah said that the reason no national railroad bill had been passed, in spite of all the grandiose schemes and flowery speeches in favor of it in Congress, was that no one had

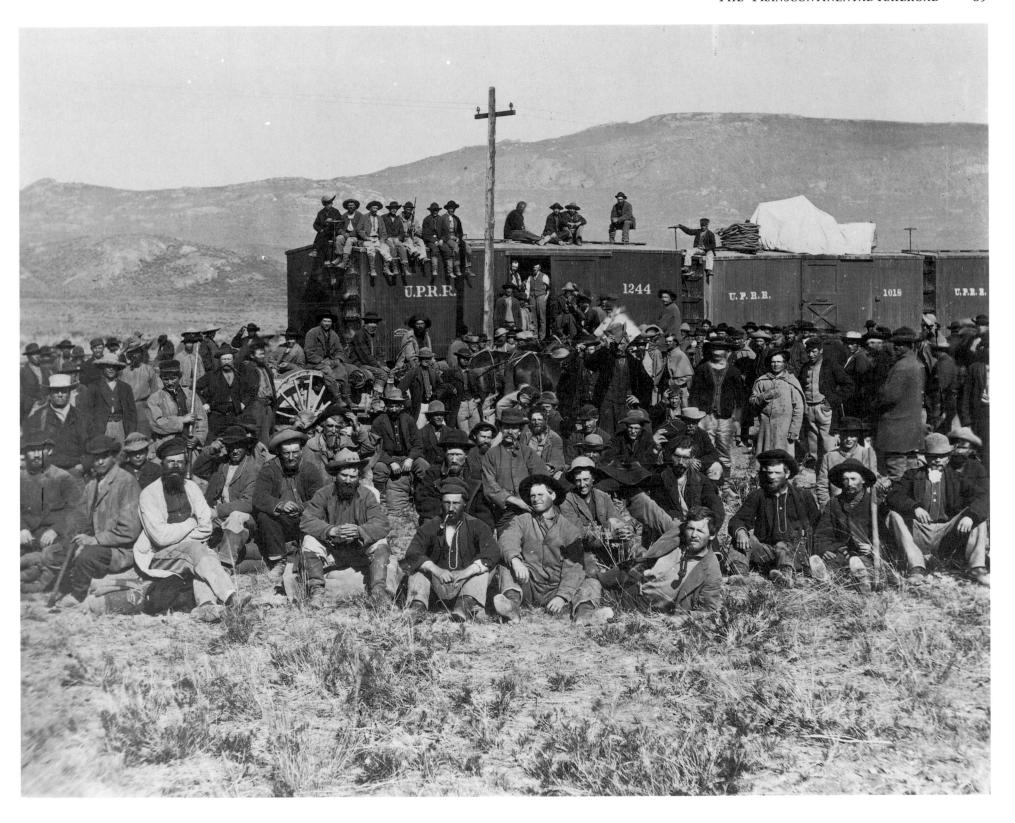

Above: This bank cut at Sailors' Spur is 180 miles from Sacramento on the Central Pacific line. CP's Chinese crews accomplished it with picks, shovels and horse-drawn dump carts.

Facing page: The Secrettown Trestle was a 90-foot-tall marvel of engineering built by Central Pacific crews.

any facts. He proposed to definitively answer any practical questions about a road to California as Congress might want to ask, giving data as to the length, alignment, grades, number of tunnels, amount of excavation, masonry needed and natural building materials available. In October 1861, having obtained the support of Huntington and the Big Four, he sailed for Washington.

Thanks to the solid engineering work of Judah and Dodge, the Pacific Railroad Act of 1862 launched a project that was both logical and well-grounded. If only the construction process had been as well considered. Judah was not always in accord with the partners on matters of policy, and they quarreled. He thought they had agreed that his services previous to the final organization would be taken as equivalent to the first 10 percent payment on his stock, but Hopkins maintained that he had no recollection of any such agreement, and the Big Four finally bought Judah out for $100,000. On his last trip to New York, where he intended to interest eastern capitalists in the project, he contracted Yellow fever crossing the isthmus of Panama and died in New York on 2 November 1863. So at the age of 37, an end came to the career of the man who initiated the California railroad, an idealist and dreamer whose enthusiasm and vigor were equal to the practical demands of the organization, promotion and lobbying necessary to bring ideas to reality. This left the Big Four.

Charles Crocker's pastor described him as a man of double character, one who was usually jolly, cheery and affable, but who could instantly become decisive and firm. Shrewd and full of guile, he kept his men from striking for more wages by suggesting to his superintendent that their pay be cut. When the Union Pacific sent a man out to see how much track could be laid in the last year of construction, Crocker and his superintendent carried on a spirited discussion about difficulties they had encountered and the lack of supplies. As a consequence, the Union Pacific man reassured his superiors by reporting that the Central Pacific could not lay 150 miles of track in a year, but it actually laid 501 miles in nine months and got the government subsidy that went with it. When the *Sacramento Union* declared the road to be unsafe over a 50-mile stretch, Crocker invited the United States commissioners to ride over it at 50 miles an hour, and be put a glass of water on the floor to show them that the track was so good, that very little of the water would spill.

It was Crocker, too, who helped move the Sierra Nevada 20 miles west, thus increasing the amount of government subsidy by $640,000. He took Professor Josiah Whitney, the state geologist, for a ride over the route, showing him a profile of the road from Sacramento to Truckee and asking him to designate the beginning of the Sierras, where the triple rate of pay from the Government began. The geologist decided that rising ground began at Arcade Creek, though the true base had generally been considered 20 miles east of this point, 'but for the purpose of the bill, Arcade Creek would be as fair a place as any.' With this data as evidence, Collis Huntington was able to get Arcade Creek officially designated as the beginning of the mountains.

As a demonstration of what he could do as a builder, Crocker organized his men to lay 10 miles of track in a day. Although the superintendent said the number required to do this was so great that they would get in each other's way, Crocker organized the work as Ford later organized automobile building, so that each man tapped only one particular spike or made one motion in laying a rail. An Army general who watched the work said, 'Mr Crocker, I never saw such organization. It was just like an army marching over the ground and leaving a track built behind them—and all done about as fast as a horse could walk.'

Above: **A Central Pacific excursion train 57 miles from Sacramento, at Cape Horn in 1867.**

Below: **The Chinese work crews chose their own cooks and tea carriers.**

Facing page: **An early Central Pacific train hauls ties across the Little Truckee River in California's Sierra Nevada.**

Mark Hopkins, the oldest of the Big Four and the one who attended to the office work, had joined Huntington in 1856 in the hardware and mining supplies business, a venture which was most successful. The firm was the symbol for all that was honest, progressive and sagacious in mercantile affairs and was a training school for young men. The association with Huntington continued until Hopkins' death in March 1878.

Leland Stanford, the partner who handled the railroad's political affairs in California, helped to organize the Republican party in California, was its first nominee for treasurer, and twice its nominee for governor, being elected the second time. As Civil War governor and the first Republican to hold the office, Stanford headed the state which contributed $178 million in gold to the US treasury. He was a liberal supporter of the Sanitary Commission, predecessor of the Red Cross. From the beginning, Stanford supported the idea of a Pacific railroad, and like the other partners, he furnished fertile soil for Judah's appeal.

At the beginning of construction, the Central Pacific was referred to as 'Stanford's moonshine project,' and the newspapers freely predicted that there would never be a railroad to Nevada by way of Dutch Flat, for the obstacles were too great. The Big Four had faith in Judah's survey and never flinched. Stanford became a political power in California, and from 1885 to 1901 he served as a United States senator. This widened a breach between him and Huntington, who, feeling that Stanford was using the railroad as an instrument for his own personal advancement, forced him from the presidency. Huntington assumed that position himself and declared that he intended to use the office to further the interests of the railroad and nothing else.

Grief-stricken when his only son died in 1884, Stanford turned his attention to the disposal of his great fortune as a memorial, which resulted in the founding of Leland Stanford Junior University, which he endowed with $20 million. The establishment of this western university with an endowment four times that of Columbia and five times that of Harvard, astonished the world, and it was doubted that California could ever furnish enough students to make proper use of it. However, Stanford soon became one of the most outstanding universities in the world.

Collis Potter Huntington was the railroad's financier and lobbyist, the strongest of the Big Four and the last to survive. With Hopkins, Huntington built up a great hardware business in Sacramento and San Francisco. In his relations with his partner he lived up to his motto 'Trust all in all or not at all.' He said, 'Not an unkind word ever passed between us. When our articles of co-partnership were drawn up, each took a copy and put it away and neither ever referred to it again.'

When Judah asked him to subscribe to his project, Huntington gave nothing, but he asked Judah to come to his office the next night, and the small group he had gathered there gave all that was needed for the surveys. A shrewd financier, he was able to carry a loan of $7 million at seven percent during the height of the Civil War, while the Union Pacific struggled under much higher rates. When Flint, Peabody & Company of Boston said they could not sell the first issue of $1.5 million Central Pacific bonds, Huntington went out on the street in Boston and sold them himself.

Concerning railroads Huntington said, 'My ideas don't agree–they don't coincide with anybody on the legislation of railroads. I think a railroad should be treated just like any other kind of property–handle it for the best of the community. Competition will regulate prices of fares and business interests. These things will regulate themselves. You cannot, in my opinion, legislate intelligently.' And he always stoutly

Above: On 10 May 1869 the Central Pacific *Jupiter* met the Union Pacific No 119 at Promontory, Utah and united the rails across the West. This photo was taken near Promontory aboard a Central Pacific locomotive on that historic day in May.

Facing page: A Utah construction camp of the Central Pacific Railroad in April 1869.

maintained that he never bought a vote in Congress, though he remarked sagely that 'If you have to pay money to have the right thing done, it is only just and fair to do it.' It was all like a game to him, a game in which he played his hand with courage and finesse. 'I like to do things,' he said. 'It has been a great pastime to me–in all my little dealings. I have got a good deal of sport out of it.'

These were the men who built the Central Pacific, and whatever may be thought of the methods by which they obtained and held a monopoly of California's railroads, it must be conceded that they had courage, imagination and tenacity of purpose. Without men of those qualities, the railroads would not have been built.

Although the Central Pacific got under way immediately, work on the Union Pacific was delayed until the end of the Civil War. On 1 May 1866, Grenville Dodge was made chief engineer of the Union Pacific.

At the outbreak of the Civil War, he had abandoned his surveying work to organize infantry companies in Iowa. He was soon given the rank of colonel, and later that of brigadier-general, and he rose to such importance that he was assigned the task of keeping open the line of communications in the Union descent on Vicksburg. Grant considered him the ablest officer in the field in railroad work and said of him: 'General Dodge, besides being a most capable soldier, was an experienced railroad builder. He had no tools to work with except those of the pioneer–axes, picks and spades. Blacksmiths were detailed and set to work making the tools necessary in railroad and bridge building; axemen were put to work in getting out timber for bridges; car builders were set to work repairing the locomotives and cars. Thus, every branch of railroad building, making tools to work with and supplying the workingmen with food, was all going on at once and without the aid of a mechanic or laborers, except what the command furnished. General Dodge had the work assigned him and finished in 40 days after receiving his order. The number of bridges to rebuild was 182, many of them over deep and wide chasms; the length of the road repaired was 182 miles.'

His military experience stood Dodge in good stead when he returned to the engineering problems of the Union Pacific, and his friendship with Grant and Sherman and acquaintance with Lincoln procured frequent favors. Since the building of the Union Pacific, aided by government grants of land and funds, was regarded at this time not only as a commercial desirability but as a military necessity that was positively essential in binding together the East and the West, Dodge was able to draw heavily upon the military establishment for troops to protect his parties against Indian raids. He also found it to his advantage that most of his men had seen service in the Army and were, therefore, trained in military discipline.

After surveying the difficult route between Cheyenne and the Laramie Mountains, Dodge entered the Laramie plains to the west. Here, because of heavy snows in winter and the lack of water, Dodge found it necessary to carry his line through the lowest possible elevation on the plains. Clinging closely to the watercourses, he constructed a line away from the high mountains, unexposed to drifting snows and accessible to the coal fields near Rock Creek.

Dodge was equally at home riding in his carriage in the Bois de Boulogne, seeking to enlist the financial aid of Paris bankers or sleeping in a pup tent pitched in the arid Wyoming hills, eating beans and bacon from a tin plate and working 14 hours a day in the rough and tumble of mountain surveying. Of course, Theodore Judah was a similar example of versatility, who alternated the luxurious life of a lobbyist in

Above: The second crossing of the Humboldt River in Nevada. The wooden buildings are workers' living quarters.

Above right: The Central Pacific's camp at Brown's Station, Nevada, circa 1868.

Facing page: A Wyoming station with Union Pacific's Engine 23 on the main track. Diamond-stacked No 23 had been shined until every brass fitting gleamed to have its picture taken at this small way stop on the Little Laramie River, 15 miles west of Laramie. Note the antlers on the headlight. No 23 is a 'McQueen' engine built by Schenectady Locomotive Works in 1868.

Washington with the hardships of surveying in the High Sierra. During his early surveys he had so little money at his disposal that his wife used to catch trout for the meals of his crew, counting it not only good sport but a valuable contribution to the party's supplies. To all these early engineers, the building of the railroad was the only thing that mattered, and they cheerfully adapted themselves to whatever the circumstances of the moment might require.

Beset by Indians, impeded by rugged mountain ranges and great stretches of country without water, Dodge and his surveyors continued to seek the shortest, easiest way to the point where his line would meet the Central Pacific. In 1868, Dodge officially reported that there were were two million acres of farmland within 200 miles west of Omaha ready for settlement; there were 1.5 million acres on the Platte River between Fort Kearney and Julesburg that could be irrigated without much expense to the company; one million acres more on the Laramie Plains; and two million acres in the Green River valley. On the tributaries of the Green River were fine forests of pine, hemlock and spruce. There was limestone for building west of Cheyenne. There were 5000 square miles of coal fields, bearing lignite, 'which burns with a bright red flame, giving off a fair degree of heat, leaving scarcely any ashes–quite desirable for domestic purposes.' There were beds of iron scattered along the route which, with the coal, could bring the West the wealth and industry that they had brought Pennsylvania in the East. There was much gold and silver in Colorado, the Black Hills of South Dakota and Utah.

It was upon such data that the directors of the railroad, sitting around a table in New York, could raise money to finance operations and lay plans for the development of

Above: CP's No 63 *Leviathan* near Deeth, Nevada. Mt Halleck can be seen in the distance.

Facing page: The marker honoring the Chinese crews of the Central Pacific who laid the record-breaking mileage in one day. The best that Union Pacific crews could do was eight miles.

traffic. From Dodge's reports they could visualize the empire that was to be, with its checkerboards of waving grain and pasture, its irrigated orchards, its coal mines and factories, its thriving cities and prosperous people. Surely the whole fate of the enterprise as an engineering project, as a commercial success and as a factor in building up the country depended on the judgment, skill and personal force of a few hardy and intrepid engineer-builders such as General Dodge.

Dodge wrote General William T Sherman that he proposed to reach Fort Sanders, 288 miles west from the head of the tracks, in 1867, and that he needed 5000 soldiers stationed east of the mountains and north of the Platte to give his workmen confidence and ensure the success of his plans. Despite the extra troops, the Indians were more than a match for the Union Pacific. From the Laramie Mountains they swooped down on the line, pulled up the surveyor's stakes, stole the horses and drove the workmen away. The situation was so dangerous that Dodge himself traveled in a heavily armored private car.

Meanwhile, the reality of the race with the Big Four had begun to set in. The Central Pacific had originally been chartered by the US government to build east through California to the Nevada line, where it would join tracks with the Union Pacific. But the wording of the charter was vague, and Congress amended it to declare that the two railroads should continue construction until their rails met. Every mile of track meant thousands of dollars in subsidies, so each road was anxious to build as long a line as possible.

When the Big Four realized that the Union Pacific was going to beat them to the Salt Lake and cut them off from potentially rich traffic, Huntington induced president Andrew Johnson's secretary of the interior to restrain the Union Pacific from building west of the eastern end of the Salt Lake. Dodge proposed that they agree to meet at Promontory on Salt Lake west of Ogden, but Union Pacific chairman Thomas Durant, with his eye on the $30,000 a mile subsidy, refused to consider any such negotiations. So both roads pushed forward as rapidly as they could.

As Dodge continued westward and the gradings of the two roads began to parallel each other, fights between the crews were frequent. However, with the support of President Grant, Dodge had the upper hand, and he told Huntington that if they did not agree on a meeting point, the government would undoubtedly step in and take charge of both railroads.

This powerful argument settled the matter. They agreed to meet, as Dodge had originally suggested, at Promontory, Utah, west of Ogden, and the Union Pacific agreed to sell the Central Pacific its graded right of way from the west at Echo Canyon into Ogden.

Even after this agreement had been reached, there was still a spirited, if not bitter, rivalry between the two roads. Newspapers began to print reports of the race. It was pointed out that a day's work often resulted in more miles of track being laid than an ox train could travel in a day over the Overland Trail. The papers would report that the Union Pacific had laid six miles of track one day, and next day the Central Pacific, in an extra spurt of speed, would lay seven miles. Thomas Durant lost a $10,000 wager that the rival road could not lay 10 miles of track in a single day.

As the roads neared Promontory, another crisis loomed when a general strike was threatened if the Union Pacific workmen were not paid their overdue wages immediately. They had already shot one foreman, hanged another and kicked a contractor out of his own camp because they were not paid. Finally Durant, on his way west for

Above: **The gold spike that connected the rails of the Union Pacific and the Central Pacific at Promontory, Utah on 10 May 1869, two days later than anticipated due to a dispute over wages–the UP workers had not been paid their wages.**

Facing page: **The long-awaited meeting of the Union Pacific's No 119 *(right)* and the Central Pacific's *Jupiter (left)* at the Golden Spike Ceremony. Shaking hands in the center are the Chief Engineer of the CP, Montague *(left),* and Grenville M Dodge, Chief Engineer of the UP *(right).*

the final construction ceremonies, was seized by workmen and held for ransom, the ransom being payment in full of all wages. Dodge wired Ames about his desperate situation, requesting one million dollars in cash. Fortunately, the president was able to obtain this, Durant was released and the Union Pacific completed its tracks into Promontory.

On 10 May 1869, the rival roads came together, and grimy workmen, leaning on their shovels, joined with state officials and railroad officers, Mormon saints, Indians, frontiersmen and camp followers in the celebration that marked the end of five years of toil.

Leland Stanford, Governor of California, came out with his party on a special train drawn by an engine christened 'Jupiter.' The party included Huntington, Hopkins, Crocker and others. There was a lively controversy over whether Durant or Stanford should drive the golden spike, but finally the Union Pacific crowd yielded this honor to the governor.

Although the project of the Pacific railway had seemed to many a wildcat scheme, the race between the roads had filled the newspapers with stories of the magnitude of the project, its future possibilities and its importance to the nation, so the whole country was agog over the driving of the last spike. Governor Stanford, with a silver sledge, drove the golden spike home into a tie of polished laurel, touching an electric wire attached to the spike which sent its impulse over the telegraph wires of the nation and told the world that the Pacific railroad had been completed. In Philadelphia, bells were rung and cannons fired. At Buffalo, thousands gathered to hear the telegraph signals, sing 'The Star-Spangled Banner' and listen to speeches by distinguished citizens.

A hundred guns were fired in Omaha, and Chicago showed its feeling in a parade four miles long. Business was entirely suspended in San Francisco, and buildings and ships were decorated with bunting, bells were rung, whistles tooted, and the town was in a furor for days.

When their engines stood head-on at the end of their respective tracks that day, the Central Pacific had constructed 690 miles of railroad east from Sacramento and the Union Pacific, 1086 miles west from the Missouri. Each engineer broke a bottle of champagne over his rival's engine, and the day ended in speeches and feasting.

Bret Harte was inspired to write his poem, 'What the Engines Said,' which read, in part:

What was it the Engines said,
Pilots touching, head to head,
Facing on a single track,
Half a world behind each back?

With a prefatory screech,
In a florid Western speech,
Said the engine from the West:

'I am from Sierra's crest;
And if altitude's a test,
Why, I reckon, it's confessed
That I've done my level best.'

Said the engine from the East:
'They who work best talk the least.
S'pose you whistle down your brakes;
What you've done is no great shakes,
Pretty fair, but let our meeting
Be a different kind of greeting.
Let these folks with champagne stuffing,
Not the engines, do the puffing.'

That is what the engines said
Unreported and unread
Spoken slightly through the nose
With a whistle at the close.

Above: 'The last wagon train' yields to the transcontinental Central Pacific *Jupiter.* It was not actually the last wagon train, but this form of transportation was obviously now obsolete.

Facing page: A Union Pacific 'pony' locomotive.

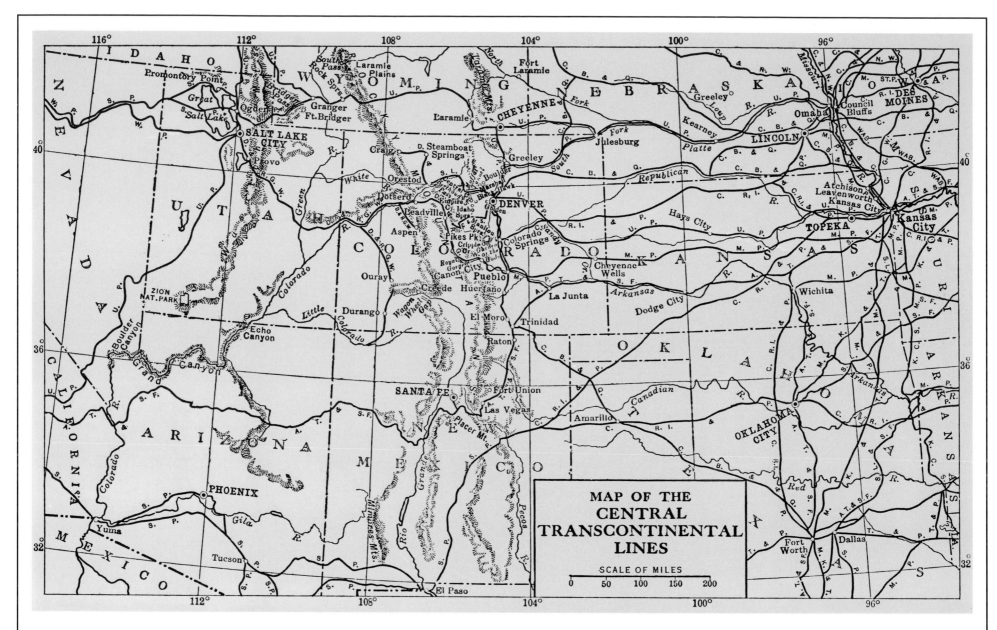

MAP OF THE
CENTRAL
TRANSCONTINENTAL
LINES

SCALE OF MILES
0   50   100   150   200

Above: This map shows the extent of the rail lines in the heart of the American West in the 1880s. Kansas City and Omaha were the 'jumping off' points, while Denver and Salt Lake were certainly now the western hubs.

Promontory, here mislabelled as Promontory Point, where the Union Pacific and Central Pacific met on 10 May 1869, is in the *upper left*. After 1870, the Central Pacific became part of the Southern Pacific (SP), which built other transcontinental lines farther south through Yuma and Tucson.

The Union Pacific (UP) built south from Salt Lake to reach the Central Pacific. The Atchison, Topeka & Santa Fe (AT&SF) reached Santa Fe in 1880 and connected its direct route to southern California in 1881. The Western Pacific (WP) crossed the Sierra and paralleled the SP into Salt Lake City. The Denver, Rio Grande & Western (DRG&W) became the essential link between Denver and the mining camps and boom towns of the Central Rockies.

Other roads seen here are the Missouri Pacific or MoPac (MP); the Chicago, Burlington & Quincy (CB&Q); the Chicago & North Western (C&NW); the Chicago, Rock Island and Pacific (CRI&P); the Missouri, Kansas & Texas or Katy (MK&T); and the Texas & Pacific (T&P).

Below: The Central Pacific's No. 1, *Governor Stanford,* a 4-4-8, is pulling into the Stanford University Museum in 1916.

The Western Bonanza

Above: **Prospectors discussing a piece of ore from their diggings in the Colorado Rockies.**

Facing page: **A miners' camp on King Solomon Mountain above Cunningham Gulch in San Juan County in Colorado Territory, as photographed by WH Jackson in 1875.**

The California gold rush that began in 1848-1849 was only the first of the many scrambles for mineral riches that hastened and justified the opening of the American West. There were many, and the next major event came a decade later in Colorado. Denver was born on 24 June 1858. W Green Russell and his party of 104 treasure-seekers from Georgia, southern Kansas and the Indian Territory camped at the point where Cherry Creek runs into the Platte River and panned some minute particles of gold from the sands. It was not much, but it was enough to keep them interested. Some days later they had taken pay dirt to the value of $400 or $500 from one spot on Dry Creek. Another party of pioneer gold diggers came after an Indian showed John Easter, the village butcher, nuggets of glistening gold which he had picked up a year before in a stream 'two sleeps from Pikes Peak.'

All pitched their tents in the vicinity of what is now Denver. Some began building log cabins, and two towns sprang up, Auraria, named after a town in Georgia, and Denver, named in honor of General James Denver, the governor of the Territory of Kansas, which in those days extended all the way to the summit of the Rocky Mountains. In 1860, the two towns merged under the name of Denver.

Even though not more than $2000 in gold was taken out that first summer, two other fifty-eighters continued the search. On 5 January 1859, George Jackson of Missouri built a fire over a frozen gravel bed on Clear Creek 35 miles west of Denver, thawed out the ground and panned coarse gold. He marked the spot, and in the spring he returned to take out $5000 worth of placer gold from Jackson Bar, in what later became the mining town of Idaho Spring. John Gregory of Georgia, prospecting several miles away, uncovered the bonanza placer ground of the Gregory Diggings, from which sprang the towns of Central City and Black Hawk, centers of one of the richest mining districts in the world.

To the people of Denver, the beneficiary of all the golden treasure taken from the Rockies round about, it seemed certain that fortune had marked their city as her own. By the law of gravity, the gold seemed to flow down the peaks and canyons of the Rockies to Denver, the goal of thousands of emigrants who pushed forward in a never-ending stream in covered wagons with 'Pike's Peak or Bust' scrawled on their canvas

Above: This street scene in Corinne in Boxelder County, Utah Territory, showing several shops as photographed by WH Jackson in 1869.

Below: This photograph of a tent town in a mountain valley in the Idaho panhandle was taken by Burt L Wheeler in November 1909.

sides. Denver soon became the commercial metropolis of the vast western plains and mountain region, and the principal city on the transcontinental route between Chicago, St Louis and San Francisco.

Despite the fact that Denver was the most lively center of population in the Rocky Mountains, the city had to bear the unkind fate of getting its mail by a stub line coming down from Fort Laramie. To improve this situation, it was proposed to lay out a stage road from Denver directly east to Leavenworth, Kansas, and the commission to do this was given to BD Williams, who later became the first delegate to Congress to be chosen by the Territory of Jefferson. This new unit of government had been brought into being in June 1859. Colorado was born when the people of the Pikes Peak district, with true, high-handed Western independence, held a constitutional convention, cut themselves off from the Territory of Kansas and declared themselves to be the Territory of Jefferson. Although Congress failed to recognize it for 21 months, the people of the Territory of Colorado lived under the rule of a hastily and questionably created provisional government, and their first delegate had the additional honor of laying out the stage route to Leavenworth.

The citizens of Denver believed that they had indeed put their city permanently on the transcontinental traffic route, for the Central, Overland, California & Pike's Peak Express Company were running 52 Concord coaches over the line from Leavenworth, making the trip in 10 to 12 days. Although there was a good route directly east, there was none to the west. When traffic ran against that massive barrier of the Rocky Mountains at Denver's back door, it had to either go north or far south to find a way through. At that time there was no road east and west by way of Denver, traversing the center of the mountain range, where the peaks were highest and most formidable.

The situation became serious when Congress, on 2 March 1861, two days after creating the Territory of Colorado, authorized the first daily Overland Mail to California, providing that mail should be carried to Salt Lake and Denver either by the main line or by branches. Clearly, this was Denver's opportunity to obtain recognition as the main stopping point on the road from the Missouri to the Pacific. It was a question whether the city should continue to be merely a branch line station, fail to fully share in the benefits of this million-dollar mail contract and allow the city to be passed by in favor of the old emigrant road through the South Pass in Wyoming. Indignant at the thought, the citizens held a mass meeting to initiate the construction of a great international highway through the heart of Colorado Territory. The mail company offered to run its main line through Denver and to the north by way of the Cherokee Trail, provided the citizens would build the necessary relay stations from Denver north to Fort Bridger. But the people of Denver did not wish to be at the lower corner of the route. They were determined to place themselves once and for all on the main line of a direct east and west passageway over the mountains, and so they did not accept the offer but turned their attention to the exploration of the Continental Divide. At their meeting, Denver and the other Colorado towns subscribed men and money, and Colorado civil engineer Captain EL Berthoud was entrusted with the task of finding a pass through the center of the Rockies over which a road could be built.

On 6 May 1861, Captain Berthoud, along with the renowned scout Jim Bridger, set out to find a pass through the center of the Rockies. Several days later, after having climbed many peaks and ridges in a fruitless effort to discover a pass, the expedition broke up into three separate parties which scattered in different directions. Berthoud says he scrambled, jumped and clambered over snowy cliffs all morning until he

Left: The Clifton, Arizona jail was built in 1881 by the Lezinsky Brothers, the original owners of the copper mines at Clifton. The contract for blasting the cells into the face of the cliff was secured by a Mexican citizen named Margarito Barela, who, ironically, was its first prisoner. He was imprisoned for a 'shooting up' celebration.

Above: A general view of the Dakota Territory gold rush town of Deadwood as it appeared in 1876 from a hillside above. Deadwood was located in the Black Hills country of Dakota Territory. Note the log cabins under construction at the foot of the hillside.

Below: This photograph of Hovey's Dance Hall at Clifton in Arizona Territory was taken in 1884. Local entrepreneur Anton Muzzonvich is seen next to the tree.

Facing page: An 1867 photograph by Timothy O'Sullivan of Orena, Nevada, showing the Montezuma silver smelting works, with the ox teams and the men at rest.

reached the summit of the divide, following the north branch of Clear Creek. Looking eastward, be saw another small creek, and after traveling four miles, he discovered that it originated from a low, even, well-defined pass, which seemed to be lower than any other point in the Colorado Rockies. On 17 May, having satisfied themselves that this offered a desirable route over the divide, the men climbed a high peak adjoining the new trail and raised the American flag.

Riding the first overland stage from Leavenworth was Horace Greeley of the *New York Tribune*, who was to become famous for his widely advertised advice, 'Go west, young man, go west,' along Albert D Richardson of the *Boston Journal* and Henry Villard of the *Cincinnati Commercial*. Villard, who would one day become one of the central figures in the success of the Northern Pacific Railroad, was a young man whom none then thought of as destined to be one of the nation's greatest railroad builders.

Greeley and Villard had come to investigate the mines, and their reports about the quantities of gold being taken out were the most valuable advertisements early Colorado ever had, as they stimulated the coming of emigrants at time when the stream lagged and many a covered wagon had returned east in disgust to spread stories of played-out mining districts, displaying a new wording of the old slogan, 'Pike's Peak and Busted!'

When he visited Denver in 1859, Greeley wrote that every guest at the Denver House 'is allowed as good a bed as his own blankets will make him. The charges are no higher than at the Astor or other first class hotels, except for liquor—25 cents a drink for dubious whiskey, colored and nicknamed to suit the taste of customers. . . . Still, a few days of such luxury surfeited me, mainly because the drinking room was also occupied by several blacklegs as a gambling hall and their incessant clamor, persisted in at all hours up to midnight, became at length a nuisance. Then the visitors of that drinking and gambling room had a careless way, when drunk, of firing revolvers, sometimes at each other, at other times quite miscellaneously, which struck me as inconvenient for a quiet guest.' Greeley also reported that there were 'more brawls, more fights, more pistol shots with criminal intent in this log city of 150 dwellings, not three-fourths of them completed nor two-thirds inhabited nor one-third fit to be, than in any community of equal numbers on earth.'

Nevertheless, the miners listened attentively when Greeley rose to address them in the barroom of this same hotel. Rotund, full-faced, with fringe of whiskers under his jaw from ear to ear, wearing large spectacles, a big, whitish, soft felt hat, a long frock coat, and baggy trousers, he was a picturesque figure. On one side 'the tipplers silently sipped their grog, on the other the gamblers respectfully suspended the shuffling of cards,' while he stood in the middle and made a strong antidrinking, antigambling speech, which was politely received.

The year after Greeley visited Denver, the city had a population of 4000, supported three daily newspapers, and boasted the Apollo theater, which seated 350, was illuminated by candles and had a one dollar admission. Five thousand acres had been staked out into building lots, and strangers were plied with investments in real estate and mines. Blake Street was said to be as lively as Broadway in New York. Farming had reached sufficient proportions that in grocery stores one might see rich yellow pumpkins, potatoes, turnips and cucumbers, sights which must have delighted the miners after their long summer in the mountains with a monotonous diet of dried beans and bacon. Adventurous young women had also begun to be attracted to the frontier. Some of them made the trip in male attire, and one advertisement asking for

Above: A miner working inside the Comstock Mine near Virginia City, Nevada in 1867. Timothy O'Sullivan took this photograph using the glare of burning magnesium for a flash of light.

Facing page: Goldhill, Nevada, looking across the town toward the mines, as seen by photographer Timothy O'Sullivan in 1867.

the services of a lad to fetch water and black boots stated that 'no young woman in disguise need apply.' Newcomers were fascinated by the bustle and adventurous spirit of the equally new town.

In these early times, the arrival of the daily Overland Mail with its passengers from the East was one of the town's most colorful events. Many other vehicles added their rattle to the din, among them the stage from Santa Fe, carrying eight heavily armed guards and 11 passengers, two of whom rode outside. The heaviest part of the traffic was carried in 'Concords' built in the New Hampshire town of that name and imitated, but never equaled, elsewhere. With no weight on the roof, they were less top-heavy than the stagecoaches. When empty, the Concord jolted and pitched like a ship in a heavy sea, but when full and nicely ballasted, its motion was easy and elastic. Its construction was so sturdy that it was said 'Concords never break down. They just wear out.' These vehicles, along with the supply wagons, pack-trains, and stages from the mines, filled the Denver streets with dust all day long.

The decisions made and the action taken in 1867 definitely determined where the future metropolis of the Rocky Mountain states was to be. The courage and energy and perseverance of the citizens of this frontier community of 7000 people literally created a city from the ground up, and they acted like a magnet in drawing the railways and trade and population that made the pioneer town a cosmopolitan metropolis. Had her people bowed before the decrees of the great Pacific railroad interests and surrendered the palm to Cheyenne, Denver might be a small town today. Even the Denver banks were establishing branches in the northern town, business was rushing there and deadly dull in Denver, and it looked as if the new town would be the future distribution point for the Rockies and Plains region.

Within a year Colorado Springs had also made much progress towards its goal of becoming a beautiful and prosperous city. Luxurious hotels were drawing tourists and health seekers to the mineral springs at the rate of 1500 a month, and the town was on the way to becoming what it was afterward called, 'The Saratoga of the West.' Broad streets shaded with trees had been laid out, parks and a sanatorium were planned, and a landscape gardener had been engaged to beautify the town.

By the 1880s, as fast as new coal, iron, silver and gold mining areas were opened up in Colorado, the Denver & Rio Grande Railroad system was extended by the building of additional branches every year until there was a network of lines running westward into the mountains. In 1882, construction began on the Rio Grande Western from Denver to Salt Lake.

Denver became the metropolis of the mountain West with the help of the railroads, but there never would have been a Denver if it hadn't been for the gold rush of 1858 and all that followed. The 1858 gold rush was nowhere near the magnitude of the California gold rush of 1848-1849, but it was, by any other measure, enormous. Prospectors poured into the gold fields by the tens of thousands. Many even left the well-worked mines of California for the richer ones—they supposed—in Colorado. No amount of hardship and suffering could deter the tide of immigration. Unwittingly, they came to lay the foundation of an empire. They were the modern argonauts, who sought only 'the golden 'fleece,' but developed the richest, fairest, grandest country on earth.

Beginning at Cherry Creek near the site of Denver, this army of prospectors scoured the plains and penetrated the Rocky Mountains searching for gold. Clear Creek Canyon, Boulder, California Gulch and many other towns 'opened rich,' augmenting

Above: In 1889, Butte, Montana, built on 'the Richest Hill on Earth,' was the third largest city west of the Mississippi.

Below: Panning for gold near Virginia City in Montana Territory, as photographed by WH Jackson in 1871.

the excitement with each increase in gold production. The discovery of silver followed, which was as unexpected as it was fortunate, opening new fields of research and bringing many more thousands of enthusiastic toilers into the Colorado Territory, which became a state in the nation's centennial year of 1876. The flood of people into the mountain towns beyond Denver was incredible. Central City–now practically a ghost town–became a metropolis in its own right.

At the same time, the prospectors were mining in Arizona, Nevada, Utah, New Mexico, Montana, Idaho and throughout the whole country between the Missouri River and the Pacific Ocean. News of rich mines in all these localities spread wildly over the land. Untold millions of precious stones and metals were treasured in the Rocky Mountain region, and the key was found with which to open the vaults. Throughout the vast territory, which the United States government had purchased from France and Mexico for about $30 million (two cents an acre), unparalleled resources in gold and silver were discovered.

This was especially true of Colorado, from whose mines alone was taken seven times as many dollars as the government had paid to France and Mexico for their claims. In the 18 months prior to 1880, the Little Pittsburg mine yielded $3.8 million; the Little Chief mine in the same period $2 million; the Chrysolite mine in 15 months $2 million; the Gregory mine $7 million in 16 years; and the Bobtail mine $5 million in 15 years. In 1885, Colorado's bullion product was $220 million, and it took the lead of all the states and territories in bullion product in 1880, with California ranking second for the first time since 1849, and Nevada third.

Although Montana was remote and isolated, it still ranked next to California in the total production of gold in the nineteenth century. The discovery of rich placer mines there in 1862 caused a rush to that region, and within three years Alder Gulch alone– 13 miles long–yielded $60 million. By 1890, Montana mines had produced, including copper and lead, $200 million worth of ore.

The gold output for 1884 amounted to $2.1 million. The silver output for that same year was $8.1 million, for a total ore output of $10.3 million.

Four large mining companies were organized near Helena in Lewis & Clark County in 1884, and others were added from month to month soon after. One contemporary writer, describing a mine near Helena, wrote: 'In point of scenic beauty, Red Mountain and its surroundings probably excel that of any camp in Montana. The beautiful Beaver Creek, leaping from its dizzy height through its narrow, rocky defile to a commingling with the waters of the Ten-mile at the very foot of Red Mountain, presents a study worthy of the pencil of the greatest artist the world can produce. Switzerland, under the treatment of the most enthusiastic writer, cannot furnish a more beautiful picture, and the entire canyon of the Ten-mile, from the Hot Springs near Helena to the source of the stream at Red Mountain, is one grand kaleidoscope of ever-changing grandeur, baffling the power of pen to describe.'

Copper, as well as gold, became an object of the miners' interest. The lodes of copper were abundant in Montana, with veins from four to 100 feet in width. Precious stones, such as agates, garnets, rubies, amethyst and jasper, were also found. A ledge of amethyst 18 inches wide was discovered on Running Wolf Creek, and a mountain of jasper near Belmont Park. Ledges of fine, white marble and sandstone of superior quality were located in Madison County. Butte, the county seat of Silver Bow County, quickly became the largest city in Montana and remained the third largest city west of the Mississippi (after San Francisco and Denver) until after the turn of the century. So

rich were the mineral deposits under Butte that the mountain it was built upon was known modestly as 'the richest hill on earth.'

Montana claimed to have the four greatest mines in the world: the Anaconda (in Butte), the Bluebird, the Granite Mountain and the Durm Lummon. Their combined product output for 1886 alone was nearly $9 million.

Meanwhile, Nevada's Comstock Lode was also yielding fabulous wealth. In the eight years between 1859 to 1867, the Comstock Lode yielded $66 million. It was thought in 1867 that this output could not be surpassed, and yet the lode in the 20 years after 1859 had a total production of $385 million, an annual average of over $19 million. The Manhattan Silver Mining Company, during just 10 months in 1884, produced 5204 tons of bullion, averaging $231.50 per ton, which was shipped to London and yielded $1,128,909.91.

The value of the bullion obtained from the Comstock Lode in 1866 was more than one-third greater than that of all the silver product of the world in 1854. In its most flourishing days from 1795 to 1810, Mexico produced an annual average of $24 million from several thousand mines. After 1810, when the revolution took place, the yield of the mines fell in some years to as low as $4.5 million. From then until the end of the century, the entire product of Mexico never exceeded that of the Comstock Lode.

Above: In 1871, WH Jackson took this photograph of hydraulic gold mining near Virginia City in Montana Territory. A flume was laid on the bedrock in the bottom of Alder Gulch and the waters of the creek were channeled through it, carrying the ore-bearing sand. The sides of the gulch were then washed away into sluice boxes where the gold was collected.

Right: The staff of the *Daily Reporter* in front of their newspaper office in Corinne, in Boxelder County, Utah Territory, as photographed by William H Jackson in 1869.

Facing page: Saloons and 'disreputable' places in Hazen, Nevada, photographed on 24 June 1905 by William J Lubkin.

Above: This display of gold bullion taken from the Union Mine on 10 January 1918 was worth $51,000 when it was photographed in Virginia City, Nevada.

Right: A panoramic view of the reduction works and copper mines at Globe in Arizona Territory, circa 1898-1899.

THE SOLDIER'S LIFE IN INDIAN COUNTRY

Above: **General George Crook's 1876 headquarters in the field at Whitewood in Dakota Territory.**

Facing page: **During the 1890s, the members of the 13th Cavalry hunted Geronimo, the elusive leader of the Apache resistance.**

When European settlers first set foot upon the shores of the New World, they were taking the first step in that relentless, ever-westward trek that would culminate in the opening of the American West. The great, unchartered land that lay before them was not, however, uninhabited. There were already a million or more indigenous people in North America. The Europeans called them Indians because they first encountered them in the islands of the West Indies, which the Europeans hoped were the *East* Indies.

Initially, the two cultures regarded each other with curiosity and occasional disagreement, but eventually–inevitably–contact precipitated conflicts. When this intercultural warfare was at its peak in the East during the eighteenth century, most Native Americans between the Mississippi River and the coast of California were either unaware of the existence of European Americans or knew about them only third or fourth hand and did not see them as a threat to their centuries-old way of life. Even in the early nineteenth century, the American government espoused this view. As late as 1821, President James Monroe recommended that the Far West, beyond the Missouri border, be devoted *permanently* to Indian use. For 15 years after 1825, with the full approval of Congress, the tribes were given homes on the new frontier. Laws were passed to protect them from encroachment, and an Indian Bureau was established at Washington to look after their needs. Indians who already lived on the plains were persuaded to welcome the emigrant Indians as neighbors as they were moved to the border from their eastern homes.

The Indian country, as it was called by law, was neither state nor territory, but a place where the Indians were colonized under special laws for their welfare. It stretched from the Red River to Canada, and from the western boundary of Missouri to the Rocky Mountains. After 1830, as the overland trails carried thousands of homeseekers and adventurers from the United States to the Pacific Coast, the western boundary of American settlement was pushed west into Indian country.

To the Indians, the trails were a calamity, for they bisected the homelands occupied by their tribes for centuries and whose sanctity had been promised to them by the US government for posterity.

From the time that gold was discovered in California in 1849 and western expansion began in earnest to the last battle at Wounded Knee in 1890, conflicts between the Indians and the white men plagued America. No simple solution was possible, given the number and variety of Indian tribal groups, the shifting US government policy toward Indians and the gap between cultures. The history of Indian wars in North America is a violent story, one marked by incidents of individual glory, cunning, treachery, courage and despair on both sides. The end of the story is already well known, but it is the struggles and battles leading up to this end that give it a lasting significance, illuminating the characters of the men who fought for their lives, their homelands and their convictions.

The decades leading up to the Civil War were marked by wars in the Pacific Northwest and lesser skirmishes, often provoked by overzealous Army volunteers, as Indians were forced to resettle in allocated territories. Installed across the frontier as a peace-keeping force, the Army had not yet geared up for major campaigns against the Indians, especially as the Civil War loomed on the horizon. At the same time, however, gold seekers formed an increasing westward flow–clothed in the guise of Manifest Destiny–disrupting the Indians' way of life. For hundreds of miles along the banks of the Platte they stripped away the grass and firewood and collected every dried-up buffalo chip for kindling. The vast buffalo herd of the Great Plains was split in two.

More than 200 fights took place in the West during the decade that followed the Civil War. New outposts and improved weaponry, combined with the strengthening of existing garrisons, brought renewed vigor into the fighting. The post-Civil War era saw mobile cavalry troops replacing slower infantry companies, and skirmishes exploded into two series of wars that were to dominate the West for a long time to come, especially in the northern plains and in the Southwest.

The soldier's life in those times was an extremely difficult one. They say that a military man's existence is characterized by endless periods of boredom and inaction, punctuated by moments of frantic, bloody and often deadly action. This was never more true than with the soldiers on the western frontier. They left the comforts of civilization in the East for the most remote corners of the wilderness, where they were expected to remain for the duration–often years–of their enlistment.

The enlisted men subsisted on rations that in some cases had been packed for use in the Civil War. They lived in horrible conditions and spent long hours in the saddle enduring the withering heat of western summers and biting blizzards of the winters. The sniper's bullet was almost a welcome diversion.

There was some pretense that the officers led a better life. In some ways they did. They had better quarters, but their food wasn't much better, and the elements and the bugs bit the flesh of a major as deeply as that of a private. The officers were, however, able to bring their wives west with them. While this may have been a morale boost for the officers, their wives found it a hellish nightmare of boredom and loneliness, where they spent most of their time gazing out the dusty windows of their homes at distant forts waiting for their husbands to return from constant, ceaseless patrols. Often, they *never* returned.

Among the soldiers, desertion was a subject of constant attention by the War Department and the country. A dozen different reasons were given for its prevalence. These ranged from ill treatment to menial employment, but is is impossible that there could be enough tyranny in the Army to cause over 3000 men to forsake their posts in a single year.

Facing page: US Army officers and their families enjoyed a delightful picnic lunch under a giant cactus near Fort Thomas, Arizona on 18 February 1886.

Above: The junction of the Mississippi and Minnesota rivers near Fort Snelling, Minnesota. The fort was the headquarters of the Twenty-fifth Infantry. This romantic 1886 view shows a young woman looking wistfully at the fort across the river.

Above: **The Fourth Cavalry's regimental orchestra paused to pose before beginning their concert somewhere in the rugged Southwest, circa 1880.**

The officers at least had the distraction of responsibility and their official duties kept them fairly well employed. The enlisted men, on the other hand, had no such attractions to keep them in the path of duty. Libraries and reading rooms were established in garrisons, but men couldn't read forever. Gambling was generally frowned upon by commanding officers, and drinking led to excess and the guard house. Drills or other duties did not take up all the soldier's time. He was up with the lark, and he had to be in bed when taps were sounded at 9 o'clock. The American enlisted soldier found himself socially ostracized, except by laundresses and 'camp followers.'

The Army on the frontier was composed mainly of recent immigrants, or the children of recent immigrants, who had not been fortunate in life. They saw the Army as being like that of the English, that is divided into two extreme classes. Its officers were marked by precedent, tradition, custom and conditions. Enlisted men, wearing an honorable uniform, rendered heroic and illustrious by a thousand victories, were regarded, although not generally treated, as serfs. At the same time, the conscripted armies of Europe, especially the French and Belgian, presented no such unfortunate condition. Summer marches, grand maneuvers, the construction of fortifications, all served to occupy the soldier's mind and to give him a higher idea of his profession, but the boredom persisted.

While the officers did not generally mistreat the soldiers, bullies were not unknown. These did not, however, last long and most succumbed to discharge, transfer or 'accidents.' Bullies were chiefly drinking officers, and sometimes they carried their offensiveness to extremes. The other officers, far from shielding them, took the very earliest opportunity of having them court-martialed. In most cases, they were

Above: **A skating party at Fort Keogh, Montana, about 1890.**

dismissed from the service, only to devote most of their lives to an effort to get back in. An unjust officer was looked upon with contempt by those above him just as he was by those under his command.

Of course, the enlisted man of the American Army was not always without faults. He frequently came from the city slums and needed to be tamed before he became a good soldier.

During the active periods, desertion was comparatively rare. The man who deserted at the beginning of an Indian campaign was indelibly branded as a coward. There were whole companies, although difficult to manage in garrison and when near alcohol, who would throw up their hats with enthusiasm when the order to march against the hostiles was given. On the other hand, there was hardly any monotony equal to that of American garrison life on the frontier during peaceful times. Officers and men assigned to small posts felt very much like they were confined on board a ship. All the acerbities and smallnesses of human nature naturally come to the surface, and a man, whether officer or private, had to be superior to ordinary human nature to stand the intolerable mental strain. The latter was always heavier on the enlisted men than upon the officers.

The boredom that everyone–soldier and civilian alike–suffered on the plains is not often recalled as being among the salient features of the legend of the opening of the American West. We remember the exciting and the glamorous, whether it is the gold rush, the cattle drives or the Indian Wars.

No person exemplified the glamorous aspect of Army life on the plains more than George Armstrong Custer. The flamboyant and colorful Custer was a legend in his own time and for more than a century thereafter. Dozens of books retold his tale in the

Above: Colonel George Armstrong Custer and Colonel Ludlow posed for WH Illingworth with the first grizzly bear that they killed during the 1874 Black Hills expedition.

nineteenth century and countless films captured visually his story in varying forms of accuracy in the century that followed.

Custer was an American folk hero and a rumored presidential candidate. He was also brash, arrogant and sadistic. He is now remembered as 'General Custer,' although he was only a temporary brigadier during the Civil War and merely a colonel throughout his career as the commander of the US Army's Seventh Cavalry Regiment on the frontier. His features were bold and aquiline. He had that remarkable gray-blue color of eyes, which may be described as liquid steel, and in his earlier military career, he allowed his abundant yellow locks to grow until they fell in profusion around his shoulders.

A heavy blonde mustache shaded his mouth and gave him a martial character. In figure, he was tall–almost six feet–and lithe, but broad-shouldered, athletic and strong. He graduated from West Point in the summer of 1861–last in his class–and immediately joined the Union Army on the banks of the Potomac.

He survived the first battle of Bull Run, and General George B McClellan appointed him an aide-de-camp on his staff. He was instrumental in discovering a ford across the Chickahominy, which enabled McClellan to make an important secret movement against Lee's army near Richmond. He served under General Philip Sheridan in the valley of the Shenandoah. Sheridan admired headlong courage in his youthful captains and promoted Custer from captain to (temporary) brigadier general when Custer was only 24.

In the fall of 1866, Custer was assigned to the Seventh Cavalry. He joined his new regiment in Kansas, which was then overrun by various armed bands of Indians, and served in that state, and occasionally in the Indian Territory, for five years. His greatest battle, except the one in which he died, was that fought on the Washita River near the Antelope Hills, in Indian Territory, on 27 November 1868. The 'battle,' which is now generally considered to have been a massacre by the Seventh Cavalry of a village filled with non-combatants, was seen at the time as a brilliant victory. Washita pitted Custer against the combined Cheyenne, Arapahoe and Kiowa tribes under Black Kettle, Little Raven and Satanta. These tribes had been troublesome to the Army for many years and they had attacked many small parties when their superior numbers assured them an easy victory.

Custer's favorite marching song was 'Garryowen,' which he used to say always harmonized with the movements and sounds of a body of cavalry charging home the enemy. Accordingly, when the time for action came, 'Garryowen' was played by the full regimental band as the Seventh Cavalry attacked. The soldiers poured their fire into the tepees from all directions, but the Indians fought back. Custer's successful, albeit brutal, attack taught them the lesson that the War Department had hoped to convey. The Washita fight was certainly Custer's most glamorous engagement and placed him in the foremost rank of 'Indian fighters.'

Custer was his own best public relations man, writing columns about himself for eastern newspapers and immortalizing himself in his book *My Life on the Plains*. His wife, Elizabeth B Custer, also painted a touching picture of her home, garrison and camp life during the later years of her husband's career in her book *Boots and Saddles*.

By the 1870s, the fierceness and tenacity of the Sioux had to be reckoned with, as the Army attempted to force them onto reservations. The climactic chapter in the conflict between the white man and the Indian began with General Sheridan's campaign in the summer of 1876, which led up to the Battle of the Little Bighorn. George Custer's

Left: George Armstrong Custer. He graduated from West Point in the summer of 1861—last in his class—and immediately joined the Union Army on the banks of the Potomac. He survived the first battle of Bull Run, and soon was regarded as a war hero.

His features were bold and aquiline. He had that remarkable gray-blue color of eyes, which was described as liquid steel, and in his earlier military career, he allowed his abundant yellow locks to grow until they fell in profusion around his shoulders. Six feet tall and lithe, but broad-shouldered, he was known as the 'boy general' but was only a lieutenant colonel during his final years.

American history might have been vastly different if Custer had won the Battle of Little Bighorn in 1876. It was an election year and there was talk of his being nominated as the Democratic presidential candidate. Rutherford Hayes won by one electoral vote (185-184), even though he lost the popular vote. As an Indian Wars hero, Custer could have swept the nation off its feet. In a debt of gratitude, the American people would have made him President. But that was not to be the case.

Above: Sinte-galeska (Spotted Tail), a Dakota chief of Dakota Territory's Rosebud Agency, was killed by Crow Dog, on 5 August 1881.

Facing page: (from left to right): Red Dog, Little Wound, John Bridgeman (interpreter), Red Cloud, American Horse and Red Shirt. Red Cloud of the Oglala Sioux spoke for the Sioux and the Cheyenne at Fort Laramie in June 1866, and ultimately refused to negotiate with the deceitful Sherman.

disastrous defeat there was the most spectacular victory achieved by the Indians during the wars on the Plains, and it was also their last major victory.

Conflict intensified in the 1870s when the Army shifted its attention to the Sioux, the one tribe—aside from the Apaches—which seemed to pose a continuing, perhaps permanent, threat to Western settlement. The Sioux leaders at that time included 40-year-old Sitting Bull, who was a master politician as well as a war chief. In 25-year-old Crazy Horse, the Sioux found a natural military genius, and because he was married to a Cheyenne, ties between the Sioux and Cheyenne grew stronger as war approached.

In 1873, Sitting Bull blocked surveys of a Yellowstone River route for the Northern Pacific Railroad. Twice Custer had to fight the Sioux. In 1874, Custer explored the Black Hills area of Dakota Territory, an area sacred to the Sioux. The Hills had been ceded to them in 1868 as their land 'forever,' part of the Great Sioux Reservation. However, some of Custer's men found gold in the Black Hills and miners began to prospect its streams by the summer of 1875. The Army removed the pioneer party of miners from Gordon's Stockade, but others followed. So many men slipped past Army patrols that a gold rush occurred as public pressure to open the hills to legal white settlement increased. The Army was soon swept aside and, to the anger of the Sioux, soon cities like Lead and Deadwood became boomtowns reminiscent of California's Mother Lode of 1849.

About 240,000 square miles were comprised in the lands ceded by the government to the Indians. The government had agreed to dismantle the military forts established along the Montana emigrant trail, running within a few miles of the base of the Big Horn Range, including Fort Reno, Fort Phil Kearney and Fort CF Smith, situated on the Bighorn River.

Finally, the desperate US government offered to pay the Sioux six million dollars for the Black Hills. Some Indian leaders were amenable to selling their holy mountains. Although they had lost them already, they wanted five times this sum. Other tribal leaders would not hear of selling their ancestral lands for any price. So, between the railroad building and the Black Hills gold rush, the Sioux drifted back onto the warpath, ignoring the government's orders to return to the reservation, and Custer was in the middle.

The Sioux and Cheyenne together were more than a match for all the other tribes combined, and they had at least 70,000 people, 15,000 of whom were able-bodied warriors. Tribes such as the Snakes, or Shoshones, and the Bannocks bordered on the Crow territory in southeastern Montana and were treated as enemies by the Sioux and Cheyenne. The abolition of the three cavalry forts excited the Sioux because the fine hunting grounds of the Crow country fell into their possession. The American government, instead of standing by and strengthening the Crow, abandoned the positions that would have held the more ferocious Sioux in check. The Crow lands were constantly raided by the Sioux. Several battles were fought, and finally the weaker tribe was compelled to seek safety beyond the Bighorn River.

The War Department sent its best man, General George Crook, to put down the Sioux and their Northern Cheyenne allies in the Bighorn country. He had 10 companies of cavalry and two of infantry. His field commanders were polar opposites—the reckless Custer and the timid Alfred Terry. On the Bozeman Trail the Bighorn Expedition found a more formidable foe than even the Sioux. A series of severe March storms lashed at the cavalry, freezing the troopers, although they were bundled up in long underwear, blanket-lined overcoats, fur caps and buffalo robes.

Above: SJ Morrow photographed cinching and loading the pack of this mule with flour during the starvation march of General George Crook's 1876 expedition into Montana Territory.

Crook's Sioux campaign of 1876 began poorly. Colonel Joseph Reynolds was defeated on the Powder River, and, unknown to the Army, the Rosebud-Bighorn country held the the greatest concentration of warriors in the entire history of America's Indian wars.

The Crook plan was to be a three-pronged attack on the Bighorn country involving Colonel John Gibbon coming from the west, General Alfred Terry and Colonel Custer from the east and Crook himself from the south.

By the time that the proud Centennial Year of 1876 rolled around, to be celebrated with a great world's fair in Philadelphia, the Sioux and Cheyenne were preparing a celebration of their own. It would show their independence of the Great White Father in the East and his Long Knives on the western Frontier. By 1876, 50,000 Indians were in rebellion. Only 15,000 were bona fide warriors, and probably no more than 4000 took the field against the Army.

General Crook, who knew the Apaches much better than he did the Sioux, was surprised on the morning of 17 June 1876 when he was attacked on the Rosebud. Only the splendid fighting of the his Shoshone and Crow allies prevented a disaster. Never was conflict fiercer than in the broken terrain, terrible for cavalry or to execute any kind of concerted battle plan. Crook was humbled by Crazy Horse. Though he admitted to only 10 dead and 21 wounded, many believed the casualty count of chief scout Frank Grouard, instead–28 killed and 56 wounded. The neutralizing of Crook by Crazy Horse, who himself had lost no less then 36 dead and 63 wounded in the fray, guaranteed Custer's utter defeat at Little Bighorn. Unfortunately, neither of the other columns learned of Crook's demise. Gibbon and Terry would eventually meet, but it would be too late to save Custer's Seventh Cavalry.

Terry issued written orders so that there would be no misunderstanding his plan. This was to bottle up the hostiles in the Little Bighorn Valley between Custer and Gibbon. However, Custer was worried that he could not catch the enemy in order to defeat him. Custer, in buckskins, leading between 600 and 700 horse soldiers, was later accused of direct disobedience of orders. There is no doubt that he bent them badly, ignoring Terry's instructions to ascend the Rosebud to its head before turning west after the Indians, whose trail had been found by Reno's scout. Such a delay would have given Gibbon's foot soldiers time to get into position to support the cavalry in the Little Bighorn Valley.

Instead, when the Indians' trail left the Rosebud for the Little Bighorn drainage, Custer followed it. This rashness compounded his initial mistake of terribly underestimating the number of his foes. A tragedy of errors was thus set in motion. He attacked at midday on 25 June 1876, choosing the single moment in history when 3000 warriors, at the very least, were gathered to fight together. Many were armed with Winchester repeating rifles against the troopers' single-shot Springfield carbines. Custer knew that the Indians had spotted him and were probably aware of his strength. However, he was completely unaware of the fact that he was outnumbered five to one. Suicidally, Custer split off three troops under Captain Frederick Benteen in a scout to the south and three more with Major Marcus Reno. The latter was to chase a party of 40 Sioux into the upper end of the village. Everything went wrong.

Reno charged as ordered, but could not make a dent in Chief Gall's huge force. There was no sign of Benteen or of Custer supporting him from the rear. Reno did the best that he could with just 112 men. He retrieved his men from the outskirts of the village, where Sioux swarmed. He dismounted in a patch of timber, but Indians

Above: Dr Valentine I McGillycuddy was both a surgeon and a topographer on march with General George Crook's 1876 expedition into the Bighorn country of Montana Territory.

Left: WH Illingworth photographed this column of cavalry, artillery and wagons, commanded by George Custer *(center, in buckskins)*, crossing the plains of Dakota Territory during the Seventh Cavalry's 1876 venture into Montana. If only he'd had this entire force intact and in one place on 25 June, history would have been much different.

infiltrated his line. Seeing a trap closing on him, he ordered his men to remount and fell back across the stream to dig in on a bluff above the river. Reno lost half of his command in dead, wounded and missing.

Meanwhile, Custer came in sight of the first village and found it to be an armed camp. He rushed a courier to Benteen, ordering him to join him and to bring extra ammunition. 'Bring packs! Bring packs!' he scribbled on the note that he gave to his orderly. Custer then charged, but soon pulled up in the face of overwhelming odds and led a withdrawal to a high grassy ridge. It was Gall who pushed him back, but then Crazy Horse struck from the north. Another force left Reno's shattered command to be in on the kill.

Benteen topped a rise and saw soldiers surrounded on a bluff. He took them to be Custer's men, so he galloped to their aid. It was actually Reno. When both officers heard shooting from downstream, they knew that Custer was also engaged.

Reno did not know what to do. Should he risk going to Custer's aid, as some of his officers insisted, now that he was reinforced? Or should he stay put in his defenses? After all, Custer was supposed to come to the support of his second-in-command, not vice versa. But Custer had ordered Benteen to reinforce *him*, not Reno. And the latter, at least on paper, had a stronger force than Custer.

Helping Custer was a forlorn hope at best. Reno's force was too battered. It was too late, anyway. Crazy Horse, apparently employing more Cheyenne than his own Sioux, had already surrounded and destroyed Custer's entire command. It took him only an hour. Crazy Horse was helped by Gall after he split his force, but easily kept Reno and Benteen pinned down while assaulting Custer at the same time.

Crazy Horse and Gall turned to destroy Reno and Benteen. They easily chased them back to their bluff. The troopers fought well to save their lives but, even in rifle pits, they suffered 18 more deaths and had 43 wounded. Enemy fire did not slacken until nightfall, when the besieged soldiers watched the enemy below them, illuminated by the glare of campfires. In the darkness, the officer and 16 men trapped in a copse of cottonwoods slipped safely through Reno's lines. With the first light of dawn, the siege was tightened. Benteen and Reno had to throw back two assaults. Bravely, Benteen led a few counterattacks to keep the Sioux and Cheyenne at a respectable distance.

That evening the Indians withdrew, setting a grass fire to screen their movements. Their scouts had spied the approaching relief column led by Terry and Gibbon. Terry had been alerted by his scouts to the disaster.

Ironically, Reno and Benteen as yet did not realize that Custer's force had been destroyed to the last man of the original 215. The Army buried the dead, took 52 wounded men in wagons and fell back to Fort Abraham Lincoln. Reno's casualties were 47 killed and 53 wounded. Estimates of Indian losses ran all the way from 30 to 300.

The shock waves of the Custer calamity rippled across the entire country from the grassy plains of Montana and Dakota to New York, New Orleans and San Francisco.

Custer's disaster, and its aftermath, drew the public's attention away from the Mexican border, which continued to simmer with violence during the last half of the decade of the 1870s. New Mexico and Arizona were ripe for trouble. Cochise, the peacemaker, had died in 1874 and General Crook had been transferred the following year. Many of the Southwest tribes had been placed on reservations, but it was soon apparent that concentrating different bands of Apaches on the San Carlos reservation

Left and above: The scene of George Armstrong Custer's last stand, looking in the direction of where the Sioux and Cheyenne village stood on 25 June 1876. A pile of bones is all that remained when this picture was taken in 1877. Colonel Myles Keogh *(above)* had been with Custer for years and their bodies were found 20 feet apart.

Facing page: Rain In the Face, of the Hunkpapa Dakota (Sioux) tribe, was captured in 1849 by Custer's younger brother Tom. After his escape, he swore to eat Tom Custer's heart and on 25 June 1876 he did.

Above: General Nelson 'Bearcoat' Miles, *fourth from the left,* and army scout LS 'Yellowstone' Kelly, mounted, at Fort Keogh, Montana as they prepare for the 1876 winter campaign against Crazy Horse.

was a disastrous bureaucratic error. It ensured the rise of the cunning Geronimo as leader of the Chiricahuas who refused to go to the agency.

The Apaches marauded more into Mexico than in the American Southwest, which did not particularly disturb the US Army. But there were enough atrocities north of the line for cavalry companies, joined by cowboy volunteers and Texas Rangers, to chase Victorio's Warm Springs Chiricahuas and Mescaleros through Arizona, New Mexico, Texas and Mexico between 1877 and 1879.

Victorio ambushed two Mexican parties in 1879 and slipped out of a trap set for him by Colonel Edward Hatch in April 1880. It was almost impossible to run him down, though he was bested–and wounded–by a company of Indian Army scouts in May of 1880.

When Victorio switched his border raiding back to the east again, he ran afoul of an almost-forgotten Civil War hero, Colonel Benjamin Grierson. The colonel surfaced quickly from obscurity by posting tough cavalrymen as guards on the critically few desert waterholes. Twice in July and August 1880 he turned Victorio back and forced him to retire into Mexico. At last, in 1880, diplomacy–and common sense–triumphed over suspicion and nationalistic jealousies. Mexico and the United States cooperated

against their common menace, Apache raiders. Victorio was killed on 15 October 1880. The old chief, Nana, succeeded Victoria although he was 70, rheumatic and had only about 15 warrior-followers.

He led the Army on another exhausting chase through New Mexico in the summer of 1881, fighting more than a half-dozen skirmishes and murdering ranchers and miners before heading westward into Arizona and Sonora to join Geronimo as his lieutenant.

There were many chiefs still active in Arizona during the 1880s, including Nana, Chato and Nachez, Cochise's son, but it was a merciless non-chief, Geronimo, who took over the leadership of Apache resistance to the increasing Anglo settlement of the territory.

General George Crook was ordered to destroy the Apache hostiles and to ignore the international boundary. Crook took the precaution of conferring with the authorities in Sonora and Chihuahua first, then penetrated the rugged Sierra Madre. His force was a small but efficient one–almost 200 Apache Scouts plus 45 Sixth Cavalry troopers. They were supported by 350 pack mules and guided by a crack Apache 'friendly' nicknamed Peaches by his Army buddies.

Above: **The US Army's Sixth Cavalry shoeing horses at Fort Bayard, New Mexico in 1885.**

Crook's patience, thoroughness and doggedness paid off. He was able to persuade most of the chiefs to give up. Chato, Benito, Loco, Nachez, Nana and even Geronimo came in, though the latter appeared to be reneging on his agreement to surrender. He did not join the others on the San Carlos Reservation until March 1884, but this arrangement didn't last. All of the chiefs, except Chato, bolted and made a run for Mexico.

Crook finally caught up to Geronimo and demanded an unconditional surrender at a meeting on 25-27 March 1886, a dozen miles below the border. Crook swore, 'If you stay out, I'll keep after you and kill the last one [of you], if it takes 50 years.' Geronimo relented and offered terms, but then changed his mind and fled.

On 1 April 1886, Crook asked to be relieved of his command. General Sheridan hurriedly replaced him with General Nelson Miles. General Sheridan ordered Miles to depend on his regulars, not Indian scouts. He did so. He also added heliograph stations to the telegraph lines to improve communications between mobile columns.

Finally, Geronimo agreed to give up, but only to Miles. The General took his surrender at Skeleton Canyon, 65 miles south of Apache Pass, on 4 September 1886, after Miles guaranteed that the Apaches' lives would be spared and that they would not be separated from their families. The prisoners entrained for Florida.

To the Native Americans and many sympathetic whites, the Battle of Wounded Knee in Dakota Territory in December 1890 was no battle at all but a massacre. In any case, it was the last major battle between the Indians and the whites. The US Army lost 25 officers and men killed, and had 39 wounded. Big Foot and his medicine man, Yellow Bird, were among the 150 Sioux dead on the frozen ground. There were another 50 Indians wounded. Probably the large number of women and children, 62, among the Sioux casualties was the result of wild firing by rifle and cannon at close quarters. In fact, some of the Army's own dead and wounded were the accidental result of gunshot and shrapnel wounds from 'friendly fire.'

By sheer coincidence, Wounded Knee occurred in the year in which statisticians of the Census Bureau declared there was no longer a line of frontier settlement in the West.

The Army was only the cutting edge of so-called civilization. It was the power behind it, the Industrial Revolution, that conquered the Indians with its railroads, barbed wire, telegraph, six-shooters and howitzers. The Industrial Revolution's agents were not only soldiers but farmers, ranchers, miners, townsfolk and buffalo hunters who utterly destroyed the Plains Indians' life-support system in one short decade.

In a sense, the Army was left to do the dirty work by others. It was usually called in at the last moment to clean up a mess made by civilians. An elderly Sioux spokesman was thinking of ordinary citizens, not troopers, when he sagely observed of the whites, 'They made us many promises, more than I can remember, but they never kept but one; they promised to take our land, and they took it.'

As historian Richard Dillon has pointed out, 'The melting pot theory of assimilation had not worked in the face of the long conflict of cultures, the clashing of races, on the plains, mountains and deserts of the West any better than in the hardwood forests and meadows of the East. So war, in place of peace, became the sorry "solution" to what was euphemized by politicians as the nation's "Indian problem." After a thousand bloody actions, in which the Army had 2000 casualties and the Indians three times that number, Teddy Roosevelt's winning of the West finally came to pass. But at tremendous cost, not only for the losers, the Indians, but also for the winners.'

Left: Geronimo, the non-chief who took over the leadership of Apache resistance in Arizona and became an arch nemesis of General George Crook.

Above: General Crook *(center)* used Apache scouts like Duchy *(left)* and Alchisay *(right)* to track and fight other Apaches. Crook was thought of as a renegade officer, but it was he who laid the groundwork for the capture of Geronimo.

Above: Brigadier General Nelson A 'Bearcoat' Miles and William 'Buffalo Bill' Cody viewing an Indian camp near the Pine Ridge Agency, South Dakota.

Above right: Captain Taylor and his noted Indian scouts on drill in South Dakota in 1891.

Right: This 1891 photo of the rifled field artillery guns was taken in Pine Ridge Agency, South Dakota.

Above left: The living gather the dead after the Battle of Wounded Knee in 1891.

Above: The dead Sioux are buried in a mass grave after the Wounded Knee Massacre, while troops look on.

Left: Big Foot, leader of the Sioux, lies frozen on the snow-covered battlefield at Wounded Knee where he died in December 1890.

Right: A photo of the Modoc Indian stronghold in northern California after its capture in the 1873 Modoc War.

Facing page: Fort McDermitt, Nevada cavalrymen pose with a cannon *(top).* The company is lined up wearing their Prussian-style helmets *(below).*

Left: During the 1880s, Indians were forced onto reservations and expected to stay put. These Crow men were taken prisoner by the US Army, who were given the task of returning them to their reservations if they strayed.

Above: A parade of US Infantry through Kearney, Nebraska in 1888.

THE COWBOYS AND CATTLE DRIVES

At right: An example of a cattle brand. This stylized illustration shows an animal that was much plumper and shorter of horn than typical Texas cattle. The Texas longhorn was the result of crossbreeding these animals with Mexican cattle. They were less beefy, but very hardy.

Facing page: A group of cowboys enjoys a storytelling session at their camp near Matador, Texas, circa 1889. Cowboy lore is an integral part of American folk legend.

With the completion of the transcontinental railroad, numerous branch lines appeared which made it possible to exploit the economic potential of the American West. This economic potential was embodied not only in the mines of California and the Rockies, but in the vast, untapped agricultural potential of what had once been the Great American Desert.

Before there were farms, crops and fences upon these plains, there was the prairie itself, an immense ocean of gently waving grassland. This was—in the terminology of the mid to late nineteenth century—the 'open range.' It was this golden land that supported the great buffalo herds—before they were killed off. In their absence, this expansive open range was perfect for cattle, which became an economically viable commodity once there were railroads to take them to the tables of easterners who craved delicious, range-fed beef.

The great herds of cattle, bred in Texas and driven north across the plains to shipping points in Kansas, Nebraska or Montana, could never have been profitable before the packing industry was developed to handle their products, or before the railroads reached the edge of the plains to carry the steers east to slaughter houses. The cattle business first appeared suddenly at the close of the Civil War. Cowboys—as the cattle tenders were called—captured the imagination of the United States and have held it ever since. Living in the saddle, riding the margin of the herds, eating from the 'chuck wagons' that accompanied them, singing the ballads of the plains and alternating long periods of loneliness on the trail with short and wild carousing in the 'cow towns' like Dodge City, Abilene and Ogallah, the cowboys became the stuff of fiction and romance. Owen Wister wrote their epic, *The Virginian.* Theodore Roosevelt, fresh from college, bought a ranch and acquired the interest that evoked his 'Winning of the West.' In 1883, from their ranks William 'Buffalo Bill' Cody recruited the staff of his Wild West Show, whose performances carried the flavor of the old West.

The cattle kingdom was a world within itself, with a culture all its own, which, though of brief duration, was complete. The cattle kingdom worked out its own means and methods of utilization. It formulated its own law, called the code of the West, and did it largely upon extra-legal grounds. The existence of the cattle kingdom

Above: **A cowboy and his horse could usually handle any emergency on the range. Here a cowboy guides a cow out of a water hole with his rope.**

for a generation is the best single bit of evidence that in the West was the basis and the promise of a new civilization unlike anything previously known to the Anglo-European-American experience.

The easterner, with his background of forest and farm, could not always understand the man of the cattle kingdom. One went on foot, the other went on horseback. One carried his law in books, the other carried it strapped round his waist. One represented tradition, the other represented innovation. One responded to convention, the other responded to necessity and evolved his own conventions.

Yet the man of the timber and the town made the law for the man of the plain. The plainsman, finding this law unsuited to his needs, broke it, and was called lawless. The cattle kingdom was not sovereign, but subject. Eventually it ceased to be a kingdom and became a province.

The cattle kingdom had its origin in Texas before the Civil War. After the war it expanded, and by 1876 it had spread over the entire plains area. The physical basis was grass, and it extended itself over all the grassland not occupied by farms. Within a period of 10 years, it had spread over western Texas, Oklahoma, Kansas, Nebraska, North and South Dakota, Montana, Wyoming, Nevada, Utah, Colorado and New Mexico; that is, over all or a part of 12 states. For rapidity of expansion there is perhaps not a parallel to this movement in American history.

It was the use of the horse that primarily distinguished ranching in the West from stock-farming in the East. The Mexicans were horsemen and the Plains Indians were horsemen. The Texans learned a new method of horsemanship and adopted new weapons in order to meet the Indians, Mexicans and the plains themselves on an equal footing.

San Antonio, Indianola, Brownsville and Laredo form the four points of the diamond. This was the cradle of the Western cattle business, filled with Mexican longhorns, Indian horses and American cowboys. This diamond-shaped region offered almost perfect conditions for the raising of cattle. The country was open, with mottes of timber offering shade and protection. Grass was plentiful, and in parts remained green throughout the year. The climate was mild, almost tropical, and there was neither snow nor blizzard, though an occasional norther swept down, only to fade and fail under the benign influences of the southern sun and the warm Gulf. The region was fairly well watered, through which ran a living stream bordered by natural parks; but, what was more important, because it was largely immune to sheltered inroads of the plains Indians.

After the 1836 Texas revolution, the Nueces valley became the scene of a border war between the Texans of the Colorado and the Mexicans of the Rio Grande. In the long run, the Texans won, and the Mexicans abandoned their ranches and much of their stock. The Texans pushed out into the cattle country and took charge of what the Mexicans had left behind. The republic declared all unbranded cattle public property, and the Texans began to convert these roving herds into private property by putting their own stamp on them with a branding iron.

It is not meant to imply that all the cattle were of Mexican and Spanish origin or that many of them were without owners. The immigrants to Texas brought their own stock, such as oxen and milk cows, and cattle were also brought in by the French from Louisiana. The bulk of the cattle, however, were Spanish. It was estimated that in the year 1830 Texas had one hundred thousand head. Four-fifths of the occupied area was stocked with Spanish cattle and one-fifth with American cattle.

Left: A round-up on the Sherman Ranch at Genesee, Kansas in 1902. A cowboy with his lasso readied looks beyond the herd toward his fellow cowpunchers waiting on the horizon.

Above: **A steer is downed for branding during an 1896 round-up in Arizona Territory.**

In 1837 and 1838, the 'cowboys' gathered herds of from 300 to a thousand head of the wild unbranded cattle of the Nueces and Rio Grande country, and drove them for sale to cities of the interior. In 1842, the driving of cattle to New Orleans began. There is a report of a drive of 1500 head to Missouri in 1842, but the earliest perfectly authenticated record of a business venture of that kind found was for the year 1846, when Edward Piper drove 1000 head of Texas cattle to Ohio, where he fed and sold them. From 1846 to 1861, the cattle drives increased. In 1850, drives began to California. The first drive to Chicago was in 1856. These early drives and sales, by land and by sea, were not only irregular but inconsequential, but the stock in the Nueces valley continued to increase. The valley became, in fact, a veritable hive from which the cattle swarmed to the north and west. An 1830 estimate gave Texas 100,000 head, the census of 1850 gave it 330,000 head and that of 1860 gave it 3,535,768 head. Each year, up to the time of the Civil War, cattle were becoming more numerous and less valuable.

The Civil War temporarily halted the development of the cattle business. A few cattle were delivered to the Confederate forces, but after the Mississippi River fell into the hands of the Union army, this outlet for Texas cattle was closed. Yet the breeding went on without abatement, and one writer maintains that the foundations of several cattle fortunes were made by men who remained in Texas while their neighbors were in the Army. Cattle accumulated; the calves remained unbranded, mingling with the old stock hardened and toughened by age. The longhorns yielded little beef and less milk, but they had a remarkable ability to survive.

An unofficial census said that by 1870, the Texas ranchers had 3,990,158 head of cattle, whereas the actual figures probably ran a million more, or approximately

Above, left: **This group of Texas cowboys signed up to drive a herd of beef cattle to Kansas.**

Above: **The cook and the 'chuck' wagon carrying food for the cowboys was indispensable in the round-ups and cattle drives.**

5,000,000 head. Cattle in Texas could be bought for $3 and $4 per head, but even so, there were no buyers. The same cattle in the Northern markets would have brought $30 or $40, and mature Texas beeves which cost in Texas $5 each by the herd were worth $50 each in other sections of the United States.

It was easy for a Texan with a pencil and a piece of paper to 'figure up' a fortune. If he could buy five million cattle at $4 and sell them in the North at $40 each, his gross profit would amount to the sum of $180,000,000 on an investment of $20,000,000 plus the cost of transportation! This exercise in high finance is, of course, fanciful, but it does show what men did on a small scale.

They took vigorous measures to connect the four-dollar-cow with a $40 market. As a matter of fact, within 15 years they actually did deliver five million head of cattle to the North, and more, though the actual profits fell short of the paper figures. At the same time, the number of cattle remaining on the breeding ground in Texas was greater than before by more than 800,000 head.

When the Texans started their rangy longhorns northward—and they were fortunate in having such tough customers for the perilous journey—they had no intention of setting up a new economic kingdom. They were merely carrying their herds to market, a market that happened to be 1200 to 1500 miles away.

Their immediate objective was a railhead from which the cattle could be shipped East. Among these roads was the Missouri Pacific, which had reached Sedalia, Missouri.

It is estimated that 260,000 head of Texas cattle crossed the Red River for the northern markets in 1866. The objective of most of these herds was Sedalia, Missouri, which offered rail facilities to St Louis and other cities. But disaster awaited the Texans

Right: The famous scout William F 'Buffalo Bill' Cody earned his nickname hunting buffalo for the Kansas Pacific construction crews.

He later earned an international reputation for his enormous 'Wild West Show,' with which he toured the eastern United States and Europe. The show earned him a fortune, and his failure as a manager lost it.

Facing page: A cook set up his gear on the back of his chuck wagon to prepare dinner for hungry cowboys working a round-up on the Box T Ranch in Texas. Erwin Evans took this photograph in the 1890s.

Below: Rath & Wright's buffalo hide yard at Dodge City, Kansas in 1878, showing 40,000 buffalo hides.

and their herds in southeastern Kansas, southern Missouri and northern Arkansas, where armed mobs met the herds with all possible violence. The pretext for this opposition was that the cattle would bring the Texas fever among Northern cattle, but in some cases, at least, robbery was the real motive.

The Texas drovers soon learned to avoid this area. Some turned to the east and others to the west, away from the bandit-infested country around Baxter Springs. Those who turned east did so in the northeastern part of the Indian Territory, driving along the Missouri-Arkansas boundary and laying their course toward St Louis or some rail point east of Sedalia. This route had few attractions. The country was timbered and broken, and the cattle reached the market in poor condition. Other drovers turned west along the southern boundary of Kansas for 150 miles until they were beyond the settlements and well out on the grassy plains. When far enough north they turned eastward, most of them reaching the railroad at St Joseph, Missouri, and shipping directly to Chicago. Other cattle found their way to feeding pens in Iowa and Illinois. To the west, some cattle went as far north as Wyoming.

On the whole, the season of 1866 was disastrous for the Texans. It was a year of groping experiment, trial and error. But it was clear that the cattle trails of the future would lie to the west. Ferocious plains Indians were preferred to the Missourians. Their future problem was to establish permanent relations with the buyers and avoid— or, better, kill, as they sometimes did—the thieves.

The man who first saw the desirability of establishing a permanent and fairly safe point of contact between the eastern buyer and Texan drovers was JG McCoy, who, with his two brothers, owned a large livestock shipping business in Illinois. McCoy, a dreamer with a practical bent, conceived the notion that there must be a strategic point where the cattle trail from Texas could rendezvous with the railroads then pushing west. Here, the Texas drovers would be met by northern and eastern buyers. 'The plan,' said McCoy, 'was to establish at some accessible point a depot or market to which a Texas drover could bring his stock unmolested, and there, failing to find a buyer, he could go upon the public highways to any market in the country he wished. In short, it was to establish a market where the drover and buyer would meet upon an equal footing, and both be undisturbed by mobs or swindling thieves.' McCoy in turn established the first cow town of the West–Abilene, Kansas. McCoy had rail connections on the Kansas Pacific to the Missouri River, and on the Hannibal & St Joe to Chicago and other markets farther east.

Curiously, the Kansas Pacific Railroad had played a role in an earlier period with livestock of a different kind. It was while the Kansas Pacific was being built that William Cody acquired his title of 'Buffalo Bill.' Cody and several other plainsmen were hired by the railroad company to provide buffalo meat for the construction crews. He was paid $500 dollars a month to kill an average of 12 buffalo a day, to oversee the dressing and cutting of the meat and get it to the construction camps where the 1200 men of the Kansas Pacific were working. The pay was high because the buffalo were already disappearing.

They had deserted the route of the railway and had to be hunted farther out on the plains. Once, when a herd of buffalo was sighted on the prairie, Cody mounted his trained buffalo horse, Brigham, and galloped away with his breech-loading needle-gun to provide the day's meat supply. When he reached the vicinity of the herd, he found five Army officers from Fort Harker waiting for the herd to pass. They told him that they would shoot the animals but wanted only the tongues and a chuck of the

Above: **The round-up pitted determined men with ropes and trained horses against ornery cattle. It was an exciting time for cowboys.**

Facing page: **The Crabtree boys and their father, with the dogs and burros with which they hunted. Their cabin was located on Long Creek, at the entrance of Hell's Hip Pocket in Brown's Basin, between Four Peaks and Salt River in Arizona Territory.**

tenderloin and that he could have the rest. He thanked them, and when the herd arrived, he ran from the party and advanced on the buffalo from the rear. There were 11 in the herd, and with 12 shots, he picked them all off before the Army officers had a chance to put their guns into action. So astonished were the officers at the prowess of this young plainsmen that they dubbed him 'Buffalo Bill,' a title which he bore ever afterward.

The Kansas Pacific had also done its part toward the destruction of the buffalo by running excursion trains filled with hunters from the Midwest, and it was not many years until the thundering herds had entirely disappeared. When the Grand Duke Alexis of Russia toured the West, Buffalo Bill was hired to be his guide in a buffalo hunt, receiving $1000 a month for his services. Needless to say, the Grand Duke shot his buffalo. In 18 months, Cody himself killed 4280 buffalo for the Kansas Pacific construction crews.

McCoy went to Kansas to select the site of his town on the Kansas Pacific. Neither Salina nor Solomon City was hospitable to the idea of being a cow town, so McCoy finally selected Abilene, the county seat of Dickinson County. Just how poor the town must have been is indicated by the fact that the saloon-keeper supplemented his income and provided himself amusement by tending a colony of prairie dogs and selling them to Eastern tourists as curiosities. The time was near when the saloon-keepers of Abilene would have too much business to stoop to prairie-dog culture. However, the presence of the prairie-dog town tells us significantly that Abilene was across the line—a town in the West.

The first herd to reach Abilene was driven from Texas by a man named Thompson, but was sold to some Northern men in the Indian Territory and by them driven to Abilene. Another herd owned by Wilson, Wheeler & Hicks en route for the Pacific states stopped to graze near Abilene and was finally sold there. On 5 September 1867, the first cattle were shipped from Abilene to Chicago. The season was late when Abilene opened for business, but nevertheless, 35,000 head of cattle found their way to this dusty cow town, and 1000 cars of cattle were shipped east. Some of the cattle went as far as Albany, New York, where 900 head sold for $300 each less than the freight charges alone.

The 35,000 head of 1867 more than doubled to 75,000 in 1868 and increased tenfold to 350,000 in 1869. It remained close to this volume until 1880, save for 700,000 in 1871 and between 150,000 and 160,000 in the 1874-1875 period.

Abilene became a symbol for all that happened when two civilizations met for conflict, for disorder, for the clash of elements of both civilizations. On the surface, Abilene was corruption personified. Life was hectic, raw, lurid and awful. The dance hall, the saloon, the red light and the revelry punctuated by pistol shots were but the superficialities which hid deeper forces. If Abilene exceeded all later cow towns in wickedness, it also surpassed them in service—the service of bartering the beef of the South for the money of the North. A good part of the nation's meat supply passed through Abilene.

It seemed like an unending stream of cattle were coming up from the South, many of them going east from Abilene or its successors, but as many more were going north and west, to supply the herds for the numerous ranches that were opening elsewhere. In addition to the five million head sent to the Kansas market and the ranges north and west, many herds were turned directly west to the ranges of New Mexico, Arizona and Colorado. Others went to Montana, Wyoming and the Dakotas and some into

Above: The legendary Judge Roy Bean holding court at Langtry, Texas in 1900. In this photo, the judge was trying a horse thief. This building was both a courthouse and a saloon. Because there were no other peace officers in the area at the time, Bean was referred to as 'the Law West of the Pecos.'

Canada. Despite this migration of cattle, the number remaining on the home range of Texas was greater than before.

The spread of the range and ranch cattle industry over the Great Plains in the space of 15 years is perhaps one of the outstanding phenomena in American history and certainly of the epoch of the opening of the American West. With it, that industry produced a culture that is the cornerstone of the epic myth of the opening of the West. In the West, a ranch covered the same area as a thousand farms, and had perhaps 10,000 head of cattle. This spawned the milieu that gave us round-ups, rodeos, cowboys on horseback and all that goes with ranching. Hot days in the branding pen with bawling calves and the smell of burned hair and flesh on the wind! Men in boots and big hats with jingling spurs and frisky horses. Camp cook and horse wrangler! The cattle were rounded up twice a year in the spring and fall. Since the range was vast and open, the round-up had to be a community enterprise in which all ranchers in the undefined territory participated. All unbranded animals were put to the iron. Cattle drives began in the fall.

The round-up was, in the truest sense of the word, the product of the open, fenceless, crowded range where men could not keep their cattle separated. The round-

up was to cattle what the harvest is to wheat–a gathering of the products of the plains grass. Branding, which followed the round-up, was merely the expression of ownership in the only way it could have been expressed.

The Western round-up in the decade 1870-1880, when the cattle kingdom was at its height and before barbed wire came into general use, often covered an area of four or five thousand square miles. The Pecos round-up of 1885 covered an area twice that size, and is probably the greatest in the history of the western cattle business.

There were two round-ups each year. The spring roundup was the more important one and was called the 'calf roundup' because it was then that the calves were branded. The fall round-up caught the summer calves and strays that the first round-up had missed. The first step in the big round-up was the meeting of ranchers at a designated place to select a round-up boss. He was a man of importance who had the confidence of the ranchers as well as the cowboys. His authority was all but absolute, and his instructions were the only law that the cowboys respected.

The primary purpose of the spring round-up was to brand the cattle, a dangerous task. Some of the men worked on horseback with a rope; others worked on the ground. The branding was done with a hot branding iron made in the form of a brand that was

Above left: The Dodge City, Kansas Peace Commissioners, photographed by Camillus Fly in 1890. *Left to right* they included Charles Bassett, WH Harris, Wyatt Earp, Luke Short, L McLean, Bat Masterson and Neal Brown.

Above: 'Black Jack Ketchum getting fitted with a new necktie' read the headline when this photograph was first published. He was hanged at Clayton in New Mexico Territory in 1901.

Above: Even in the 1890s the cowboy had become a mythic figure, symbolizing individuality and courage.

Facing page: The cattle trails of the American West began on the plains of Texas and Montana. Most terminated at rail heads in such newly successful cow towns as Wichita, Abilene and Dodge City in Kansas.

The oldest trail was the Texas Road (1), also known as the Osage Trace or Shawnee Trail. The most famous trail, and that which probably saw the most head of cattle, was the Chisholm Trail (2). The Western Trail (3) paralleled the Chisholm and one can imagine that the two often overlapped as the huge herds made their way north. Farther west, the Goodnight Loving Trail (4) served the Rio Grande Valley and Colorado.

The California Cattle Trail (5) brought fresh Texas beef to the hungry miners in the Sierra and to the tables of San Francisco until the Golden State developed an indigenous cattle industry that could satisfy the demand. Today, Texas is still the nation's largest cattle producing state. California is third behind Oklahoma. The Jones & Plummer Trails (6) came in from the north, and the Oregon Cattle Trail (7) generally followed the old Oregon Immigrant Trail into the Northwest. The Northern, or Montana, Trail (8) also served the Northwest.

stamped into the hair and hide of the animal. After they had rounded up and branded the cattle, the cowboys would drive them to meet the railheads for shipment east. Later drives, and the longest ones, were for the purpose of distributing stock cattle on the northern ranges or for carrying food to reservation Indians. The drives had had their origin in Texas before the Civil War, and the postwar disparity of prices of cattle in Texas and in the North, growing out of the prosperity of the North and the great surplus of cattle in Texas, caused a resumption of the drive and gave it an impetus that it might not otherwise have had. Before they came to an end in 1890, the drives presented a spectacle like nothing ever seen in America since the movement of the millions of buffalo across the plains. Cattle were the trail-makers, both because of their cleft hoofs, which cut the sod, and because of their habit of walking in single file.

In 1868, the businessmen of Abilene sent out a surveyor who ran a direct line between that cow town and the Arkansas River, crossing at Wichita, Kansas. This was called the Abilene Trail. But with the movement of the railheads west, the trail tended to shift west and to become shorter.

The Chisholm (pronounced Chisum) Trail was one of the best-known of the later trails. Following Jesse Chisholm's track came thousands of herds, and the trail became well known. From 200 to 400 yards wide, beaten into the bare earth, it reached over hill and through valley for over 600 miles, a chocolate band amid the green prairies, uniting the North and the South. As the marching hoofs wore it down and the wind blew and the waters washed the earth away, it became lower than the surrounding country and was flanked by little banks of sand, drifted by the wind.

West of the Chisholm was the Panhandle Trail, leading to Kansas and Colorado, and the Pecos Trail, leading up the Pecos River valley into New Mexico and on to Colorado and Wyoming. Quite naturally, cattle going to market took the most eastern trails, and those going to stock the ranges took the more western ones. As a matter of fact, there were scores of trails. In Texas the trails converged to the main highways north, and when they passed above what is now Oklahoma they diverged. They may be likened to a short section of rope with both ends badly frayed. There were trails of cattle, some of them doubtless 'wet stock' from south of the Rio Grande, and they ended in northern Montana and in Canada. Of course some of the trails diverged westward from Texas, as did the Panhandle and Pecos routes. Beyond Kansas the trails were ordinarily known by the destination, as were the Montana Trail or the Wyoming Trail.

In some ways range life was idyllic. The land had no value, the grass was free, the water belonged to the first comer and all a man needed to 'set himself up' in the business was a 'bunch' of cattle and enough common sense to handle them and enough courage to protect them without aid of the law. However, far-sighted men must have seen that things could not go on as they had been. Single outfits claimed 'range rights' over territory as large as Massachusetts and Delaware combined. It could not last.

In 1862, the Federal Homestead Law was passed; in 1874 the first piece of barbed wire was sold in the United States. These two facts combined to break the even tenor of the cattleman's way.

Until 1873, the establishment of cattle ranches in the West proceeded without interruption. Until 1870 the herds sent to Abilene and other railheads sold on a steady or rising market. Prices were particularly good in 1870, with the result that the drive from Texas in 1871 was the greatest in history, with 700,000 head going to Kansas alone. Along with the Texas cattle, the other Western states were beginning to

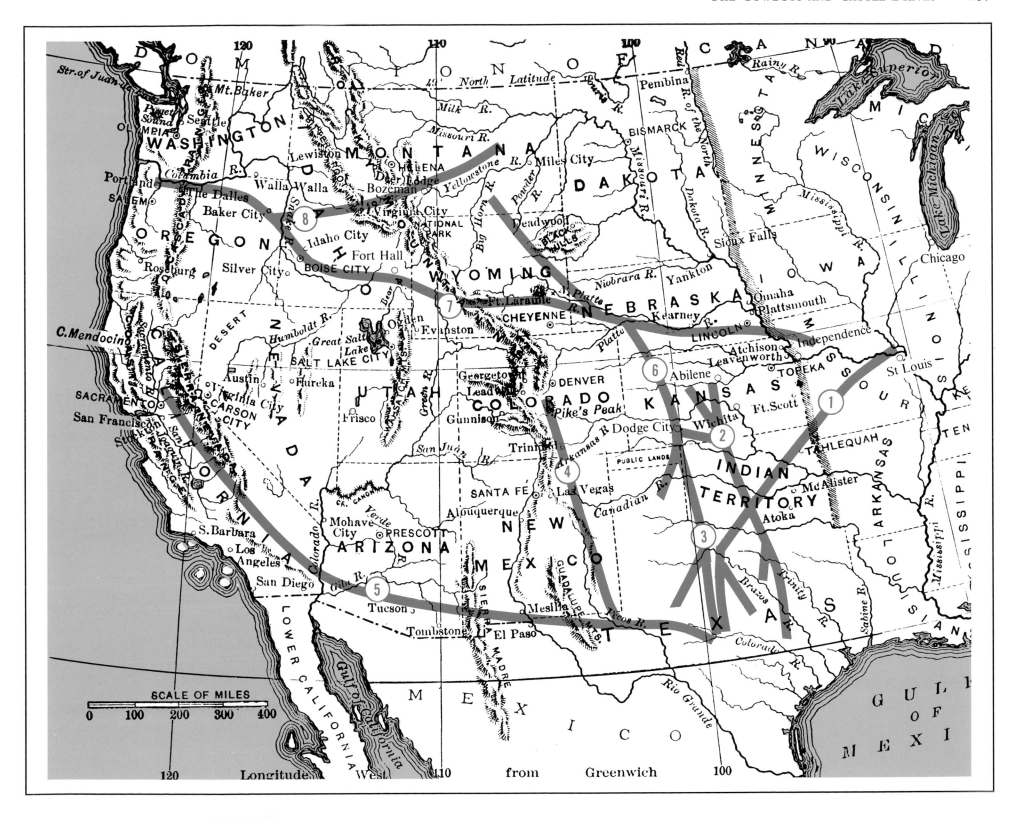

Above: **The huge herds would travel from Texas to the cow towns in Kansas, where buyers would purchase and ship cattle by boxcar to their markets in the East.**

contribute to the beef supply and to reap the benefits of the high prices. But in 1871, the market conditions had changed, and drovers found almost a complete reversal of the situation of the year before. There were few buyers, and they were reluctant rather than eager purchasers. Business conditions had slackened, the currency issue had agitated the country, and the railroads had put an end to a rate war which up to that time had benefited the cattlemen. Half the cattle brought from Texas remained unsold and had to be wintered at a loss on the prairies of Kansas. The drive from Texas in 1872, therefore, was only about half the size of the one in 1871. In Texas the situation in 1873 was bad. The corn crop promised a poor yield, the northern ranges did not need stock cattle and market demand was weak. The climax was reached on 18 September 1873 when the New York banking firm of Jay Cooke & Company closed its doors, precipitating the Panic of 1873.

By 1876, the cattle industry was recovering from the panic of three years before, and there was a steady demand for cattle, with a rising market. During the last four years of the 1870s, the cattle business expanded on a steady or rising market. In the 1880s, two million head were marketed. A well-matured northwestern ranger would bring about $60 in northern markets, and a Texas steer about $50. Grass was still free, as was the range. Then came the great boom of the early 1880s. It was said to be a time of golden visions in a blaze of glory that led to the rim of the crater of ruin—a brief era of wild extravagance. There were many factors which contributed to the boom, but given the boom, a collapse was inevitable.

As a result, the whole world (that is almost literally true) stampeded to the Great Plains to get a ranch while ranches were to be had. Easterners, Englishmen, Scots, Canadians and even Australians flocked to the plains to become ranchers, to the amusement of the cowboys and the disgust of the ranchers, to both of whom cattle-raising was just an ordinary way of making a living on horseback rather than on the ground or in an office building.

With the scramble for ranches and the improvement of national financial conditions, the price of cattle again began to rise. In 1878 and 1879, ordinary range stock sold at $7 or $8 a head by the herd, range delivery. By the end of 1880, the price was about $9.50, and by the end of 1881 it was $12.

The winter of 1881-1882 was mild in the West, and at the end of it cattle were in unusually good condition. High prices and the realization by some of the wiser cattlemen that the days of free grass and open range were nearing a close resulted in an overstocking of the range. The resulting demand led to large purchases, to a diminution of the market supply, to an increased demand for beef and finally to a continual rise in price. Range cattle were selling for from $30 to $35 per head by 1882, and cattlemen could expect a profit of 300 percent on what they had bought three years earlier. By the summer of 1882, the boom was at its height.

By 1885, overstocking the range had so reduced the grass that either a drought or a hard winter would bring disaster. One ranch near Fort Worth, Texas, had 25,000 cattle on a range of 100,000 acres. In the spring of 1883, the round-up brought in 10,000 head and 15,000 dead cattle on the range told the rest of the story. The drought was more severe in Texas than elsewhere, but it was fairly general throughout the range country. Cattle prices began to weaken in 1884, and the crash came in the next year. Cattle that had once been valued at from $30 to $35 on the range sold for only $8 or $10, if they sold at all. Prices continued to decline until 1887, when the best grass-fed Texas steers brought only $2.40 per hundred pounds on the Chicago market.

Above: **These Aztec Land & Cattle Company cowboys were photographed at Holbrook, Arizona Territory by FA Ames.**

Men who could not fence opposed the practice of fencing, clinging to the sinking ship of free grass. Cattlemen became divided into two hostile camps: free-grass men versus big-pasture or fenced-range men. The free-grass men learned the use of wire-cutters and began to cut the fences. They were not completely without justification, for their stock were sometimes terribly mutilated by the barbed wire. Then came the farmer, hated by both free-grass men and wire men alike. The collapse of 1885 converted ranching from an adventure into a business, which it is today.

Both the great cattle drives and the cowboys who were their central players presented an image that fired the imagination. A haze of romance enveloped life in the West and made the western man a legendary figure. The reality was almost as magnificent as the myth. The cowboy's life was conditioned by cattle, and every part of it was adapted to cattle. It was an expansive occupation, covering enormous areas of land. The distances in the cattle country were so great that a man on foot was helpless, if not actually in danger. The population of the range was very sparse and society was highly rarefied.

Where population is sparse, the laws are withdrawn and men are thrown upon their own resources, and courage becomes a fundamental and essential attribute in the individual. The western man of the old days had little choice but to be courageous. The germ of courage had to be in him. Where men are isolated and in constant danger or even potential danger, they will not tolerate the coward. They cannot tolerate him, because one coward endangers the whole group. The great distances and the sparse population of the West compelled and engendered self-reliance. A process of natural selection went on in the cattle country as it probably did nowhere else on the frontier.

COWBOY LORE

During the first half of the twentieth century, a time when some of the men who had experienced the West were still alive, there was a deep fascination with cowboys. From the 1930s until the 1960s, Western movies were a staple of Hollywood studios. During the first decade of television–the 1950s–half of the dramas were Westerns. This trend had ended by the early 1970s, but the late 1980s witnessed a revival of cowboy lore in the form of an interest in cowboy poetry. With this in mind, it is interesting to look at some original cowboy songs, penned a hundred years before and part of the American legend for many years thereafter.

Men have always sung at their work, especially those who work alone a great deal. The cowboy found singing a part of his occupation, a necessary accomplishment of his trade. Singing seemed to soothe the cattle and distract their attention from sudden noises that might otherwise cause them to stampede. Out of this necessity, this desire to sing, grew cowboy ballads.

THE DYING COWBOY

'O bury me not on the lone prairie,'
These words came low and mournfully
From the pallid lips of a youth who lay
On his dying couch at the close of day.

He had wailed in pain till o'er his brow
Death's shadows fast were gathering now;
He thought of his home and his loved one nigh
As the cowboys gathered to see him die.

'It matters not, I've oft been told,
Where the body lies when the heart grows cold;
Yet grant, O grant, this wish to me,
O bury me not on the lone prairie.

'O bury me not on the lone prairie
Where the wild coyotes will howl o'er me,
In a narrow grave just six by three,
O bury me not on the lone prairie.

'O bury me not,' and his voice failed there,
But we took no heed of his dying prayer;
In a narrow grave just six by three
We buried him there on the lone prairie.

Yes, we buried him there on the lone prairie,
Where the owl all night hoots mournfully,
And the blizzard beats and the winds blow free
O'er his lowly grave on the lone prairie.

THE CHISHOLM TRAIL

Come along, boys, and listen to my tale,
I'll tell you of my troubles on the old Chisholm trail.

    Coma ti yi youpy, youpy ya, youpy ya,
    Coma ti yi youpy, youpy ya.

Oh, a ten-dollar hoss and a forty-dollar saddle,
And I'm goin' to punchin' Texas cattle.

No chaps, no slicker, and it's pourin' down rain.
And I swear, by God, I'll never night-herd again.

Last night I was on guard, and the leader broke the ranks,
I hit my horse down the shoulder and I spurred him in the flanks.

The wind commenced to blow, and the rain began to fall,
It looked, by grab, like we was goin' to lose 'em all.

I herded and I hollered and I done very well,
Till the boss said, 'Boys, just let 'em go to hell.'

We rounded 'em up and put 'em on the cars,
And that was the last of the old Two Bars.

I'm on my best horse, and I'm goin' at a run,
I'm the quickest shootin' cowboy that ever pulled a gun.

I went to the wagon to get my roll,
To come back to Texas, dad-burn my soul.

I'll sell my outfit just as soon as I can,
I won't punch cattle for no damned man.

    Coma ti yi youpy, youpy ya, youpy ya,
    Coma ti yi youpy, youpy ya.

GIT ALONG, LITTLE DOGIES

As I walked out one morning for pleasure,
I spied a cow-puncher all riding alone;
His hat was thrown back and his spurs was a-jingling,
As he approached me a singin' this song:

    Whoopee ti yi yo, git along, little dogies,
        It's your misfortune and none of my own.
    Whoopee ti yi yo, git along, little dogies,
        For you know Wyoming will be your new home.

Early in the spring we round up the dogies,
    Mark and brand and bob off their tails
Round up our horses, load up the chuck wagon.
    Then throw the dogies upon the trail.

It's whooping and yelling and driving the dogies;
    Oh how I wish you would go on;
It's whooping and punching and go on, little dogies,
    For you know Wyoming will be your new home.

Some boys go up the trail for pleasure
    But that's where you get it most awfully wrong;
For you haven't any idea the trouble they give us
    While we go driving them all along.

When the night comes on we hold them on the bed ground,
    These little dogies that roll on so slow;
Roll up the herd and cut out the strays,
    And roll the little dogies that never rolled before.

Your mother she was raised way down in Texas,
    Where the Jimson weed and sand burrs grow;
Now we'll fill you up on prickly pear and cholla
    Till you are ready for the trail to Idaho.

THE END OF THE RAINBOW

T he picture on the facing page both literally and figuratively represents the end of the rainbow, the farthest extreme of westward migration across the continent. It also represents the arrival of American civilization at the Pacific shore. Actually, San Francisco had been an outpost of civilization long before Congress declared the West 'won' in 1890, and as such it served as the literal–or at least figurative–end of the rainbow that inspired the opening of the American West.

The West was a region which demanded new institutions or a radical modification of old ones and which developed a different outlook on life. Life in the West–both urban and rural–was very different from that in the East. The explorations and long trails to Santa Fe, Oregon and California, and the whole round of life in the range and ranch country inevitably found a place in the picture. Western people developed something special in their outlook on life that became the subject of the novelist, artist and film maker. Something distinctive and uniquely American was discerned.

The frontier experiences on the Great Plains were *not* a repetition of frontier experiences in the region from which the settlers came. A frontiersman from the woodland region found many new experiences.

Changes in modes of transportation marked the stages of development in the opening of the American West. From Lewis and Clark's canoes, transportation evolved through the covered wagon to the stagecoach to the railroad and finally to the automobile. Much could be said about the paramount importance of the horse in the opening of the American West. The Spanish introduced this animal to the Plains Indians, and the horse in turn brought about a complete revolution in the habits of the Indians. It was the cowboy, however, who brought the horse to the height of its power and glory in the white man's life on the plains. Man and horse were one in the cattle country. At the time the horse was playing such an important role in the West, the East was developing the railroad to supplement other forms of transportation.

A careful examination of the railroad map of 1860 will show that the most westward railroad had reached St Joseph, Missouri. The map of 1890 shows that east of the Mississippi the country had become a network of roads which extended in crisscross fashion in every direction. West of the line there were still few roads, and they were for

Above: **This Texas cattle ranch is typical of those which dotted the American prairies from the Rio Grande to the Canadian border.**

Facing page: **Against a backdrop that includes the Cliff House and Seal Rock, a family goes for an outing on San Francisco's Ocean Beach in 1902.**

Above: **The GL Rule family at their farm in Arizona Territory, where they settled in 1893.**

the most part very straight, lacking the crazy-quilt pattern that had evolved in the East. The three transcontinental roads went as straight from the Mississippi Valley to the Pacific coast as topography would permit. There were very few roads running from north to south.

By 1890, the railroads had transformed American life on the plains. They had made changes in American civilization there comparable to the changes made by the horse in the life of the Plains Indian. They had provided a means of communication and transportation over large areas. Not only did they provide transportation, furnish manufactured necessities and carry surplus products to market, but they literally and figuratively sold the land to eastern immigrants in large quantities and on terms which appeared to be very liberal. The result was a flood of immigration to the West, with each immigrant intent on acquiring land.

As the tracks had pushed forward over the prairies, that boom psychology which was an outstanding characteristic of the West and of westerners began to put forth many blossoms. While the most solidly founded town developments were made by the railroads themselves or their subsidiaries, there were many independent real estate promoters who were willing to guess where the roads were to establish division points and to dream rosy dreams of the future possibilities of any city site where land could be

obtained, however unfavorable it might be. It was no trouble to build new cities on paper.

In 1862, Congress passed the first Homestead Act. This permitted any citizen over 21 years old or any head of a family to acquire 160 acres of public land by giving legal notice of his intention (called 'making entry'), then living upon the land for five years and making certain improvements. Later laws provided for homesteads up to 640 acres in semi-arid regions or where the soil was poor. Land was cheap. The Homestead Act permitted anyone who was interested to ride into the West, select a claim, erect four posts around a hollow square on the ground and file a notice in the land office that he had laid the foundation of a house and begun settlement.

Once the land was patented, it could be sold to an incorporated town site company, which itself could stake out 320 acres of government land as a town site, and by adding surrounding homestead claims could increase its holdings to a thousand acres or more. Then the land would be cut into building lots, usually 25 by 125 feet, and a selling campaign begun. If the town was a success, the promoters grew rich. If it failed, little was lost, for the land cost but a trifle. In 1867, there were a number of such towns in Kansas: Wyandotte, four months old, population 400, with shares of 10 building lots selling for $1800; Doniphan, 1500 acres, population 300, with shares selling at $500;

Above: **The first blacksmith shop opened in Guthrie, Indian Territory, in 1889 soon after the area was opened to homesteaders.**

Above: **The Hancocks turned over the first sod on their homestead near Sun River, Montana on 5 November 1908.**

and Geary City, where shares had advanced from $250 to $400 within a week. And the residents of each embryonic metropolis, as well as the promoters thereof, could give unanswerable arguments as to why their community was to be the future St Louis of the territory.

The various gold rushes had brought people to the West who intended to strike it rich quickly and go back to the East. Some went back, some stayed on. The difference between the gold rushes and the land rushes was that most of the people who went west for land planned to stay. This was, in a sense, the ultimate drama in the opening of the American West.

Those who settled in the West began to discover riches that a quick pass with a miner's pan could never have revealed. There were riches that would be manifest only after a growing season or two. In the Dakotas (derived from Dakota Territory to become states in 1889), farmers learned that the days, by reason of the higher altitude, being longer and cool nights, favored the cereal crops. They had the deep frosts, which gradually melt and supply moisture to growing plants and less intense heat during the maturing months, which make possible the production of hard spring wheat—a cheap crop by reason of its being a quick-growing crop that takes only 100 days to mature

Above: **A little girl feeding chickens on the Hancock homestead near Sun River, Montana in 1910.**

after seeding. The prevailing westerly winds, called 'Chinook,' extend to the inland plains of the northern Pacific country and sensibly modify the climate.

In New England, the farmer waits for the frost to be gone before he undertakes planting seeds. But in the Dakotas, and all through the region which the Northern Pacific Railway opened for settlement, the farmers planted and sowed as soon as the warm sun of March melted three or four inches of the six feet of frost in the soil.

A pioneer farmer from New Hampshire rented an 80-acre farm in Meagher County, Montana in 1870 on which there was a small log cabin and a barn. Without capital and with but one team, he raised 2400 bushels of wheat, which he sold for enough money to enable him to purchase the farm, pay off some old debts and settle his family there. The other crops he raised were soon sufficient to pay hired help and incidental expenses, so that the barley crop yielded a net profit.

Another farmer, in Gallatin County, Montana, began in a small way, gradually enlarging his farm as the sale of his crops enabled him to make purchases, until, at the end of 10 years, his farm embraced 680 acres, all of which he fenced and divided into mowing fields and pastures. Although Montana had 22 million acres of heavy forest, the territory also had well over 16 million acres of land suitable for cultivation,

Above: Anadarko Townsite in Oklahoma Territory on 8 August 1901, showing an auction in progress in a lumber company booth. Temporary bank buildings and the beginnings of a 'lodging house' can be seen nearby.

and in 1880, Montana stood at the head of the list in the number of bushels of wheat, rye and oats raised per acre. The average was over 26 bushels to the acre. Its closest competitors were Washington Territory (23 bushels to the acre) and Colorado, which produced 22 bushels. The national average was only 12 bushels per acre. Colorado contains five million acres of agricultural lands with deep, rich soil, located mostly in the valleys of its great rivers–an area about the size of Massachusetts.

By and large, however, the land on the plains–which only a few years earlier had been 'the Great American Desert'–had yet to reveal its immense agricultural value. In contrast, the land in California's rich valleys had immediately proved to be the equal of the placer mines of the Golden State's mountains. From almost the time of the 1848-1849 gold rush until after the Great Depression of the 1930s, California was considered to be more than simply the land at the end of the rainbow; it was a veritable Garden of Eden.

Between California's two mountain ranges–the Sierra Nevada and the Coast Range–lies a rich, fertile valley, which was once an inland sea. It is 80 miles wide, hundreds of miles long and contains over five million acres of splendid land. While the average rainfall is sufficient to assure good crops, irrigation has been extensively introduced to increase production. By 1890, California was being called the 'cornucopia of the world.' Grains and fruits of every sort and even tropical fruits seemed to grow luxuriantly there.

The pioneer found that fruit trees seemed thrive much better in California than they did in New England. Apple trees begin to bear at three years of age, and the peach at two. The plum and cherry trees grew larger, bore fruit much earlier and their fruit was found to be less perishable than kindred fruits in the East. A California farmer's orchard might be found to have apple, peach, pear, cherry, prune, quince, plum, nectarine, pomegranate and fig trees. In Oregon and California both, strawberries and

Above: A teacher and her class in front of a sod schoolhouse in Woods County in Oklahoma Territory, as photographed in 1895.

Above: This photograph, originally captioned 'Champagne Corking,' was taken by Eadweard Maybridge at the Buena Vista Vineyard in Sonoma, California during the 1870s. It shows a shed where disgorging, perfecting the fill and recorking were carried on. The man inspecting the labeled bottle is BE Auger, who was for many years an officer and trustee of the Buena Vista Viticultural Society.

The building at the rear is the brandy distillery. The Buena Vista Winery is still one of California's premiere establishments.

Facing page: In the 1880s, California had become one of the major exporting states. The Golden State's railroad network would bring wine, lumber, wheat and other products to the Pacific Coast, where they would be shipped to markets around the world.

other berries could be produced in every month of the year. The orange, lemon, lime, almond, olive, English walnut and apricot trees flourished in southern California.

Wine-making soon became one of the leading industries of California, with business expanding at a remarkable rate within a few short years. By 1890, the annual yield was 10 million gallons, and rapidly increasing.

Farmers used to the concept of spring and winter wheat found that there was no such distinction in California because of the year-round growing season. Grown in California, it simply becomes California wheat. In Liverpool, or any other market in Europe, it was quoted as white wheat, with the highest prices.

The scene to the north of California in Oregon and Washington represented a similar story, albeit on a lesser scale. The Willamette Valley in Oregon and the Yakima Valley in Washington offered an agricultural bonanza very much like that of California's vast Central Valley. In the woods of Oregon and Washington were the most magnificent forests of fir, many of them so enormous in bulk as to suggest the Redwoods of Yosemite and the northern California coast. This lumber region furnished a large part of the commerce of Puget Sound, and the lumber business grew to immense proportions. At the same time, salmon fishing on the Columbia River was one of the most remarkable industries of the West.

The pioneers who participated in the opening of the American West came for the adventure, they came for the gold, and they came for a new life. It was hard, and it was often not what they had expected. Yet somehow, an all-new breed of American founded an all-new American dream, creating their own pot of gold at the end of the rainbow.

Above: In the early 1900s California logging railroads flourished up and down the Pacific Coast, running cut logs the short trip to the mill.

Facing page: The Northwestern Pacific Railroad operated many of the logging railroads in the redwood country of California's northwest coast. These redwood sections were harvested for use in building San Francisco's Victorian homes, most of which were built in the 1870-1910 period. Redwood is still the building material of choice in northern California because of its resistance to the sort of moisture damage that ruins pine lumber.

Above: Not the Heartbreak Hotel on Lonely Street but rather the Wild West Hotel on Calamity Avenue in Perry, Oklahoma Territory, in September 1893. One cannot imagine a heartbreak greater than checking into this hotel.

Left: Nogales in Santa Cruz County, showing the boundary line between the United States territory of Arizona and Mexico's state of Chihuahua. WJ Newman's 1898 photograph was taken from a hillside looking west along International Street.

Right: Two Mormon women and their small children pose at a dairy building in what was later known as Mormon Lake, Arizona. They were photographed by FA Ames, who worked in the area between 1887 and 1889.

Facing page: A comfortable Montana ranch photographed by WH Jackson in 1872.

Holding Down A Lot In Guthrie.

26

Above: Would-be homesteaders holding down a lot in Guthrie in Indian Territory (later Oklahoma), as seen by photographer CP Rich in 1889.

Facing page: This enterprising entrepreneur was in the furniture and undertaking business on Broadway in Round Pond, Oklahoma Territory.

Right: The English Kitchen on Broadway in Round Pond, Oklahoma Territory, offered meals for a reasonable price. Quality was commensurate.

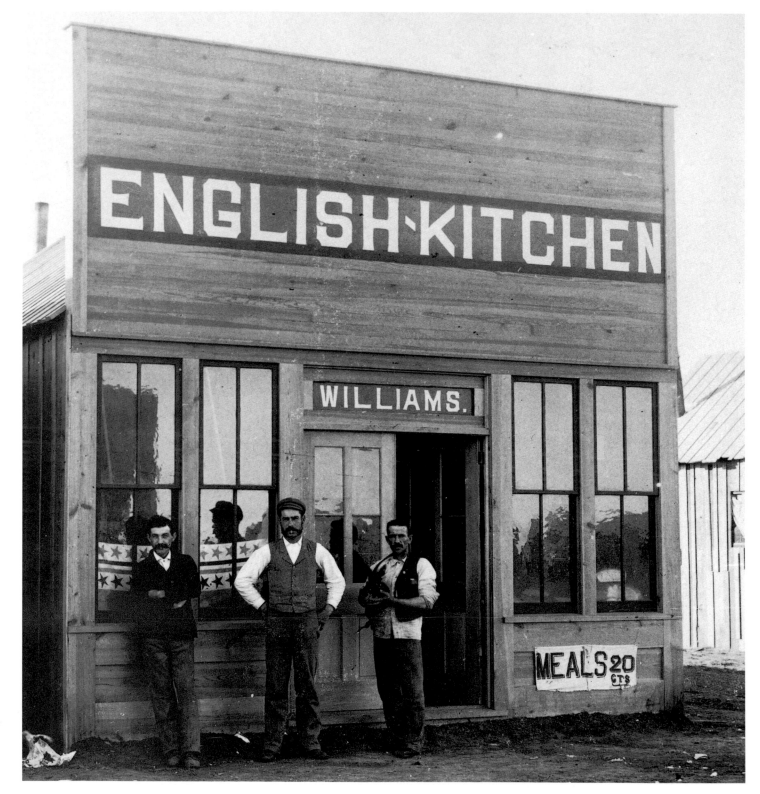

Facing page: Attorneys and surveyors posed in front of their office west of Courthouse Square in Round Pond, Oklahoma Territory for Robert Kennett in January 1894.

EPILOGUE

Above: Two Oldsmobile runabouts line up in New York City for a race to Portland, Oregon in 1905. The 44-day trip covered 4000 miles of crude roads, and the winner, 'Old Scout' *(left)*, outraced 'Old Steady' *(right)* and arrived for the opening of the Lewis and Clark Centennial Exposition.

Facing page: A covered wagon with 'jackrabbit' mules encounters an automobile on the trail near Big Springs, Nebraska.

T he opening of the American West was an epic of immense proportions. An indomitable people had settled a land the size of Europe in more or less a century. It was the stuff of legends, and indeed, it created legends by the thousands.

What if the great migration had been the other way—west to east? What if the same hand that had guided the Pilgrims to Plymouth and to the rock-bound shores of the Atlantic had led them instead to the gold-fretted shores of the Pacific? Perhaps for those fearless, self-sacrificing, intelligent, hardy people disciplined by perils and hardships indescribable, rocks were better than nuggets of gold. A soil that would yield bread enough to keep the wolf of hunger from the door only by a constant 'sweat of the brow' was indispensable, rather than a soil that would yield the necessaries of life and luxuries of the tropics in profusion, with little care and labor.

Had the Pilgrims landed at San Francisco instead of Plymouth and the treasure vaults of California had been opened by their enterprise in 1620 rather than 1848, would there have been an 'opening of the American East' in the nineteenth century or before? Or after? Finding a rich soil that yielded crops with a fraction of the labor required to secure a subsistence on the coast of New England, the goading incentive to work or starve would have been removed. Generations lived and died before the opening of the West was thought to be possible.

The opening of the American West was a singular experience. Nothing like it has happened anywhere on earth since perhaps the days 200 centuries ago when the ancestors of the Native Americans first arrived from Asia.

In the 1890s, Andrew Carnegie wrote: 'The old nations of the earth creep on at a snail's pace; the Republic thunders past with the rush of the express. The United States, the growth of a single century, has already reached the foremost rank among nations, and is destined soon to out-distance all others in the race. In population, in wealth, in annual saving and in public credit, in freedom from debt, in agriculture, and in manufactures, America already leads the civilized world.'

All this being true, when did the opening of the American West end? When was the American West finally open? Congress declared an end to the frontier in 1890, but the

Above: Members of the Denver Motor Club test-driving the Denver-to-Salt Lake 'Exposition Route' near De Beque, Colorado. Photographed by AL Westgard in 1912.

Facing page: The highways of the United States in 1923 were still mostly just partially-paved roads. It would not be until 1935 that it was possible to drive from coast to coast on a *paved* highway.

The names were colorful but were seen in the 1920s to be less efficient than the number system introduced in 1926. The most famous was certainly the Lincoln Highway, which gave way to US Route 40 and finally to Interstate 80. The National Park-to-Park became US Route 99 and eventually Interstate 5. The old Oregon Trail had many names as a highway but was numbered as US Route 30 and now is Interstate 84. The old Santa Fe Trail became part of the nation's most storied numbered highway–US Route 66–which itself was superseded by Interstates 40, 44 and 55.

last Indian who died at Wounded Knee was not buried until January 1891. Custer had died in 1876, but Geronimo lived until 1909.

The answer to the question probably lies in the technology of the transportation used by the pioneers who *opened* the American West. Lewis and Clark used canoes because they thought that means of transportation would be faster than horses. Subsequent expeditions came on horseback and the horse became synonymous with the plains and mountains of the West. The horse (as well as the oxen) pulled the wagons of the people who came to stay, and the stagecoaches that followed after real road had been built. Even when the railroads changed everything, their locomotives were still referred to as the iron *horses*.

At the dawn of the twentieth century, the West was changing and so was the technology of travel. No single innovation would affect the technology of travel more than the automobile and Henry Ford's ingenious means of getting them into the hands of large numbers of people. After 1903, there was no turning back. The Ford Model T suddenly gave the individual American a power of transportation never before available. By the teens, the automobile was omnipresent in the cities of the East and Midwest, as well as on the highways and byways of the Atlantic seaboard. San Francisco also echoed to the sputter of automobiles, but nobody drove them to California from Detroit. It was an all-new era in the transcontinental migration of Americans. It was the final era in the opening of the American West.

The West would not be open, truly open, until it was possible to drive in an automobile from New York straight through to San Francisco on a *paved road*.

It is indicative of the pioneer spirit of the people of the West that the first successful transcontinental car trip on *unpaved* roads *began* in San Francisco. On 23 May 1903, Dr Horatio Nelson Jackson and Sewall K Crocker drove east from the University Club on San Francisco's Nob Hill in an open-topped Winston touring car in response to a $50 bet made the week before. On 25 July, they drove down the Hudson River from Peekskill and entered New York City. The hardships they endured were many. There were few roads between the Sierra Nevada and the Mississippi River, and they were scarcely better than they had been when wagon trains crossed the plains. Yet they had succeeded in an accomplishment that was of no less importance than the first trek by John C Fremont or the meeting of the rails at Promontory.

There would be several other crossings over the next few years, but these pioneers were considered as crazy–if not more so–than the pioneers of 80 years before. It was a stunt–celebrated in events like the transcontinental Curved Dash Race of 1905–but not considered practical. The first woman to make the trip–without the company of a man–was 21-year-old Alice Huyler Ramsey, who drove from New York to San Francisco in a 30 hp Maxwell in 1909. She suffered numerous flat tires and breakdowns, and at one point was forced to fix a broken axle. Three female companions who accompanied her on the venture watched as Ms Ramsey made all the repairs herself.

In 1904, there were 78,000 automobiles in the United States, but only seven percent of America's rural highways were surfaced. Almost all of them were in California or the East. By 1918, there were 5.6 million automobiles, but little improvement in the proportion of paved roads. The idea of a practical, paved transcontinental highway was an obvious dream.

It was Carl Graham Fisher, a Miami developer and bicycle racer, who, in 1912, launched the first campaign for a transcontinental highway. He quickly secured the support of tire and automobile manufacturers (except, curiously, Henry Ford), and of

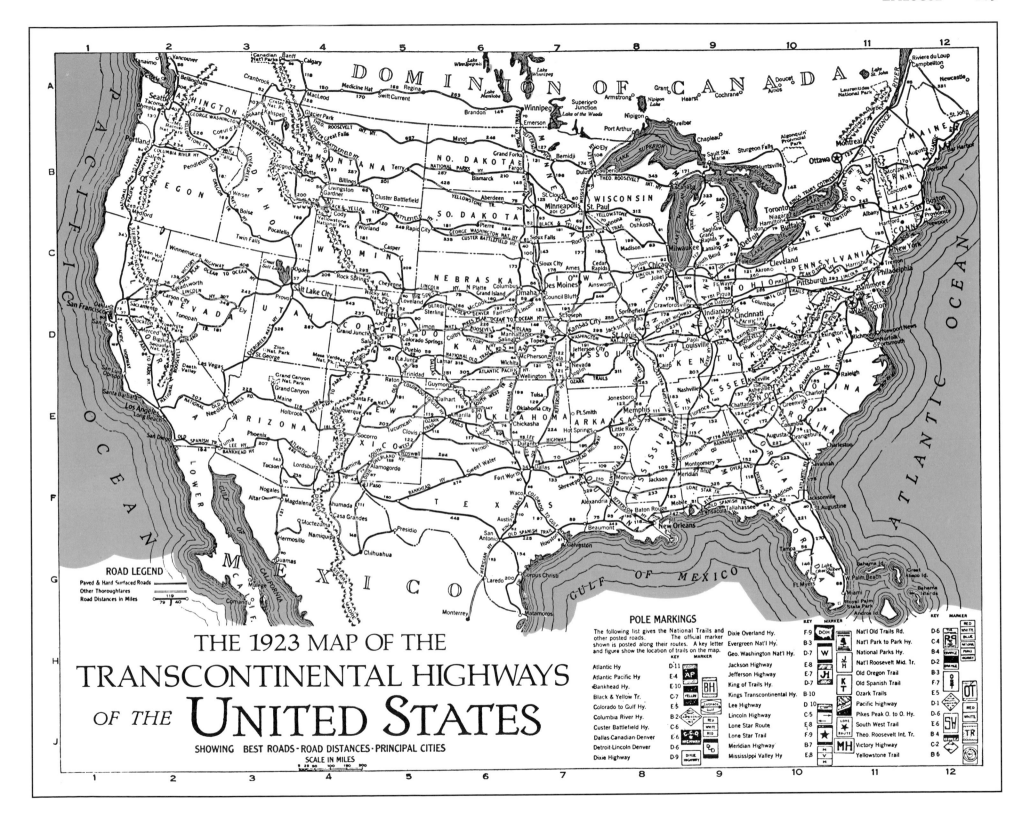

THE 1923 MAP OF THE
TRANSCONTINENTAL HIGHWAYS
OF THE UNITED STATES
SHOWING BEST ROADS · ROAD DISTANCES · PRINCIPAL CITIES

ROAD LEGEND
Paved & Hard Surfaced Roads
Other Thoroughfares
Road Distances in Miles

SCALE IN MILES

POLE MARKINGS

The following list gives the National Trails and other posted roads.   The official marker shown is posted along their routes.   A key letter and figure show the location of trails on the map.

	KEY	MARKER
Atlantic Hy	D-11	
Atlantic Pacific Hy	E-4	AP
Bankhead Hy.	E-10	BH
Black & Yellow Tr.	C-7	YELLOW
Colorado to Gulf Hy.	E-5	Colorado Gulf
Columbia River Hy.	B-2	R U
Custer Battlefield Hy.	C-6	WHITE RED
Dallas-Canadian-Denver	E-6	C-C-D HIGHWAY
Detroit-Lincoln Denver	D-6	D C D
Dixie Highway	D-9	DIXIE HIGHWAY

	KEY	MARKER
Dixie Overland Hy.	F-9	DOM
Evergreen Nat'l Hy.	B-3	
Geo. Washington Nat'l Hy.	D-7	W
Jackson Highway	E-8	JH
Jefferson Highway	E-7	JH
King of Trails Hy.	D-7	KT
Kings Transcontinental Hy.	B-10	
Lee Highway	D-10	
Lincoln Highway	C-5	
Lone Star Route	E-8	
Lone Star Trail	F-9	★
Meridian Highway	B-7	MH
Mississippi Valley Hy	E-8	

	KEY	MARKER
Nat'l Old Trails Rd.	D-6	RED WHITE BLUE
Nat'l Park to Park Hy.	C-4	THE NATIONAL PARKS
National Parks Hy.	B-4	
Nat'l Roosevelt Mid. Tr.	D-2	
Old Oregon Trail	B-3	
Old Spanish Trail	F-7	OT
Ozark Trails	E-5	
Pacific highway	D-1	
Pikes Peak O. to O. Hy.	D-6	RED WHITE
South West Trail	E-6	SW
Theo. Roosevelt Int. Tr.	B-4	TR
Victory Highway	C-2	
Yellowstone Trail	B-6	

Above: Photographer AL Westgard was on hand to capture this scene as towns-people in Ehrenburg, Arizona Territory, greeted a stranger in an automobile on his cross-country tour in 1911.

Facing page: In 1923, this Oldsmobile, driven by racer 'Cannon-ball' Baker, made the transcontinental trip from New York to Los Angeles in record time—12.5 days. To keep the car in high gear, all other gears were removed from the car.

the newly-formed American Automobile Association. In the spring of 1913, the Lincoln Memorial Highway Association was formed in Detroit to build a highway of the same name. It was to begin at Times Square in New York City and proceed westward to the Pacific Ocean at the west end of San Francisco's Golden Gate Park, at the end of the four-mile, four-lane boulevard still known as Lincoln Avenue.

The Lincoln Highway, a milestone at its conception, was soon overshadowed by the highway boom of the 1920s that saw the creation of the Theodore Roosevelt Highway, the Yellowstone Highway, the Dixie Highway and highways named for both the Atlantic and Pacific oceans. There were, in fact, so many confusingly *named* highways that the US government introduced the *numbered* highway system that is so familiar to all of us today.

When the numbered highway system was officially adopted on 11 November 1926, it encompassed a national highway system that was 96,626 miles long, yet *none* of the highways was continuous from coast to coast!

US Highway 40, which was the designation given to most of what had been built as the Lincoln Highway, was largely, but not completely, paved. US Highway 30, which was intended to run from Philadelphia to Salt Lake City and then follow the old Oregon Trail to Astoria, was in a similar state of incompletion.

Amazingly, it would be almost another decade before the dream was complete. On 24 October 1935, Harry Dixon of the Chamber of Commerce of North Platte, Nebraska, sent a telegram to President Franklin D Roosevelt, which read in part: 'US Highway 30 will be the first hard-surfaced, all-weather road connecting the Atlantic seaboard and the Pacific Coast. The last link of 30 miles near our city will be completed and ready for opening and dedication of the entire route on Tuesday, 5 November at two pm Central Standard Time. Elaborate ceremonies here. Eleven governors along highway are invited. Some have accepted. Others will participate in various ways. National publicity given the importance of this federal-aided project. We ask that you cooperate by pressing an electric button in Washington to sever the golden ribbon to be climax of ceremonies and officially open this great highway. Arrangements have been completed to place at your convenience the necessary equipment and connection for the honor you will do us in complying.'

Steve Early, the assistant secretary to the President, replied on 24 October 1935 that the president would be in Hyde Park on 5 November and that there were no facilities there he could use to hook up and press a button for the dedication. He did, however, offer to provide a message from the President for the occasion.

Dixon replied by telegram on 31 October 1935 that he would be pleased to have a message from the President 'on completion of the longest hard-surfaced highway in the world' and that it would be read at the ceremonies on 5 November.

The President's message to Dixon was dated 1 November 1935 and read: 'Completion of the last link of pavement on United States Route 30 is an event of such importance that I am happy to send my congratulations. The perilous trail of the pioneers is at last transformed, by joint efforts of the federal and state governments, into a coast to coast highway. With full appreciation of the manifold benefits of this modern avenue of communication, it is especially gratifying to recall that its construction has been a part of the great program of highway building that has given needed employment in recent years to hundreds of thousands of our citizens.'

The West was open.

Right: Nevada City, California, is a testament to the people who caught 'gold fever' and came west to the gold fields of the Sierra Nevada.

The buildings in this 1924 photo were already more than 50 years old when the first gasoline engine rattled down these winding streets. Most of these buildings still exist.

Facing page: Plymouth, California, another gold rush town in El Dorado County, in the early 1920s. Its Main Street was never paved with gold.

INDEX